Red Sky at Night

Books by VERNON OICKLE

1993
Life and Death After Billy

Friends & Neighbours: A collection of stories from The Liverpool Advance

1997
Busted: Nova Scotia's War on Drugs

1999
Queens County (photo book)

2001
Ghost Stories of the Martimes

2001
Dancing With The Dead

2002
Ghost Stories of the Martimes Vol. II

2003
Great Canadian Ghost Stores Vol. II

2007
Disasters of Atlantic Canada

2008
Canada's Haunted Coast

2008
The Editor's Diary: The First 13 Years

2010
Angels Here Among Us

One Crow Sorrow

Red Sky at Night

Superstition and Wives' Tales by Atlantic Canada's Most Eclectic Collector

By Vernon Oickle

Published by
MacIntyre Purcell Publishing Inc.
232 Lincoln St., PO Box 1142
Lunenburg, Nova Scotia
B0J 2C0 Canada
www.macintyrepurcell.com

We acknowledge the support of the Department of Canadian Heritage and the Nova Scotia Department of Communities, Culture and Heritage in the development of writing and publishing in Canada.

Printed and bound in Canada by Transcontinental.

Library and Archives Canada Cataloguing in Publication

Oickle, Vernon L.
Red sky at Night : superstitions and wives' tales compiled by
Atlantic Canada's most eclectic collector / Vernon Oickle.

ISBN 978-1-926916-10-1

1. Superstition--Atlantic Provinces.   2. Folklore—Atlantic Provinces.
I. Title.

GR113.5.A8.O53 2011   398'.4109715
C2011-903246-5

*Dedicated to the memory of my grandmother Pearl
and all those superstitious people in the world*

Table of Contents

Introduction

Growing up in rural Atlantic Canada, I was fortunate enough to be exposed to beliefs, traditions, superstitions and customs that today may seem to belong to a bygone era. My grandmother was, I think, the most superstitious person I've ever known. She held tightly to what she called the "old ways." It was her way of seeing the world, and. for me, a product of postivism of the pubic school system, it was an antidote to rigidity of that system. She engendered in me a life-long love and respect for and interest in superstition.

Superstitions are part of our heritage. These traditions are hand-me-downs from our forefathers and they are an important part of our legacy. They permeate our everyday existence, often on a subconscious level.

Everyone knows that you touch wood for good luck, right? Or that it's bad luck to spill salt, or that you must never whistle on board a ship because it will bring on a bad storm. You know that, right? Sure you do. Often times, you just don't realize how superstitious you truly are and those of you who do realize, don't really want to admit it or dismiss it.

It is unfortunate, but our attention to and speculation about phenomena has dissipated with the advent of science and technology. We no longer observe the skies or the subtle changes shown to us by Mother Nature, but rather depend on the the observations of experts. We consume rather than participate.

Ancient cultures around the world were awake to the possibilities the world around them represented. Although many of those beliefs have been debunked or contextualized by today's science, what has been lost today is that sense of awe and wonder and connection that our ancestors were fortunate to have.

Storms and lightning, early arrival of animal life, the volume of rain or snow were not events to be endured so much as a natural cycle of life. The universe was a place of give and take. For me, it is a way of being part of world, not apart from it. It is respect for that way of being that is lost today.

Over the years, I've maintained a collection of these superstitions as my way of staying connected to my grandfather and grandmother and to the world they represent to me. I'm excited about the chance to share many of them in this book. I thank all of those who contributed to this effort by sharing their superstitions. Their kindness and knowledge have made this book a reality. Thanks also to publisher, John MacIntyre, for having faith in this unusual topic.

—**Vernon Oickle**
If you have superstitions you want to share, reach me on facebook at:
www.facebook.com/redsky2011
Twitter: www.twitter.com/redskyatnight1

"As infants, our first victory comes in grasping some bit of the world, usually our mother's fingers. Later we discover that the world, and the things of the world, are grasping us, and have been all along."

— Stephen King

Chapter 1

Animal Antics

The living world has had an enormous influence on superstition throughout the centuries. Newcomers to Atlantic Canada brought their beliefs with them and by so doing have enriched the mental landscape that is still with us today. They carved new lives out of what was virgin land. They joined an already rich heritage of myth and mythology that were and are part of First Nations living.

The role animals have played and continue to play form an important function in the mythology of Atlantic Canada and the world beyond. Animal myths are common elements in our literature, film and storytelling. Passed down from generation to generation, they have gained a foothold in the landscape of our minds.

Let's take a look at the burrowing groundhog, an animal largely forgotten, except on February 2nd. Groundhog Day is when the world checks in to see if the furry little rodent might show his face. If you are anything like me, you, too, tune in to see whether there will be six more weeks of winter if he should see his shadow, or whether there will be an early spring. The legend of the groundhog actually dates back to the 18th and 19th centuries in Germany and first came to North America via Pennsylvania. Today, Groundhog Day has practically become a national holiday with festivals, marching bands, banners and a full day of celebrations in many places.

Nova Scotians have anointed Shubenacadie Sam as its chief weather prognosticator. Other famous groundhog meteorologists include Wiarton Willie and Gary the Groundhog in Ontario, Brandon Bob in Manitoba and Balzac Billy in Alberta. The granddaddy of them all is Punxsutawney Phil from Pennsylvania.

Growing up in Liverpool, I was surrounded by superstition - and it wasn't just groundhog forecasters that played a part in my upbringing. I have an uncle who believes that dogs are among the most astute weather forecasters. He believes that if a dog sleeps facing north, it means there is a bad winter storm brewing. His old mongrel, more than just his faithful companion, has never gainsaid his belief. I was and still am mesmerized by my uncle's predictions and his ability to talk about them.

My grandmother, who ran a small hobby farm with her husband in Queens County, was one of those who believed that a solitary crow was a harbinger of doom and gloom. My grandfather maintained that if the spring's first calf is breached, then it is a bad omen for the rest of the year.

When I hear these beliefs dismissed off-handedly as merely nothing more than "superstitions" or "old wives' tales," I am reminded how close our forebears lived with nature and just how much of that we've lost in the modern age. Perhaps the current state of the environment stems from that lost connection. The following may reawaken your ability to look at animals in a new light.

A MOUSE IN THE HOUSE

We're not talking Mickey here. We're talking omens of misfortune.

- If a mouse was discovered in the house, it was thought that someone in that house would soon die.

- In another version of this belief, a mouse in the house could foretell a terrible tragedy such as an accident or fire.

- It is bad luck to bury a dead mouse in your yard because nothing will ever grow there again.

The exception here is:

- You should allow your cat to kill as many mice as it can, because with every mouse it kills, it also kills one of your enemies.

- If a cat brings a mouse to your house, then it means no one in your house will go hungry.

DOWN ON THE FARM

Find out what certain things mean when they occur down on the farm.

- If a calf is still-born, someone on the farm will die.

- A white calf born in the winter? Prepare for a harsh weather.

- A cow that doesn't give milk for a week is a sign of a harsh winter.

- If a cow is milked outside the barn while it is standing on the ground, the animal will dry up.

- If you sing inside the barn, the cows will not give milk.

- It is good luck to have a cat in your farm to say nothing about keeping the mice population under control.

THE SKY IS FALLING

This may be something to cluck about

- If the hens don't lay eggs for three consecutive days, it's a sign that a tragedy is about to befall the farm.

- If the hens nest in the morning, it's a sign of impending death, usually that of the farmer or someone in the family.

- A hen or rooster getting inside the farmhouse predicts a visitor that day.

Did you know...

that a horseshoe hung in the bedroom will keep nightmares away?

HORSING AROUND

Sorry to nag you, but these four-legged creatures have a lot to say about what's going on in your life.

- Horse brasses were used to protect horses from witches.

- Changing a horse's name is bad luck.

- Inhaling a horse's breath is said to be a cure for whooping cough.

- If a horses stands with its back to the barn door, it is going to rain.

- A horse that neighs at the door of a house is a sign of sickness for the inhabitants.

- If you break a mirror, the misfortune can be averted if you lead a horse through the house.

- If you walk under a ladder it is considered bad luck but you can avoid the bad luck if you keep your fingers crossed until you have seen three horses.

- The tail of a horse is adorned with ribbons to keep the animal safe from witches.

- Dreaming of a white horse is considered a death omen.

- Gray horses or horses with four white feet are considered unlucky.

Did you know...

that if a mouse is discovered in your house, someone is thinking bad thoughts about someone who lives there and may wish them harm?

- If you wear a hair from the tail of a black stallion on your wrist you will be protected from witches.

- It was thought that warts could be cured by circling them in horsehair.

- If you lead a white horse through your house, it will banish all evil.

HORSESHOES KEEP YOUR GOOD LUCK UP

Remember to hold the good luck in.

- A horseshoe nail is frequently used as a good luck charm if it is bent into a circle by a blacksmith.

- A horseshoe, hung above the doorway, will bring good luck to a home.

- Witches fear horses. They avoid a door with a horseshoe mounted on it. The horseshoe must be hung with the points up to keep the luck from spilling out.

MAN'S BEST FRIEND

Does your dog have a sixth sense?

- It was once believed that if a dog howled for no obvious reason, something tragic was about to happen.

- If a dog passes gas, it's a sign that a bad storm is coming.

- When a dog buries its bone in your garden, it indicates a poor harvest that year.

- A dog barking at the door of your home, but there is no one there, means the spirit of the recently deceased has visited your house.

Mary Jane Lamond

Mary Jane Lamond is a sharer of songs, stories and spirit. This sharing has garnered Lamond numerous Juno and East Coast Music Award nominations as well as critical acclaim and a worldwide audience. Mary Jane's latest recording, "Storas" (Gaelic meaning "a treasure"), is a beautiful interpretation of some of the Scottish Gaelic songs that have become part of Nova Scotia's Gaelic tradition. On the North Shore of Cape Breton Island, the rich heritage of the region's Scottish settlers was kept alive through song. It was in Nova Scotia, visiting her grandparents throughout her youth, that Lamond fell in love with Scottish Gaelic traditions and song.

Living in the Gaelic community of Nova Scotia I have, of course, encountered lots of examples of superstitions and beliefs: An droch shuil (the Evil Eye), An Da- shealladh (second sight); traditionally in this culture, fairies, forerunners and ghosts abound. More than one storyteller has certainly convinced me that we share our world with many creatures we cannot always see.

I would say that my main fear in the superstition area is "the jinx," that is saying something will be good before it happens. I just about have a heart attack when someone in the band says something like "This is going to be a good show tonight." To me, that just about guarantees that absolutely everything that could go wrong now will. I think that by announcing a certain positive outcome somehow you just open the door for everything to be negative. It's not that I believe that the opposite is true. I don't think that making negative statement makes things better, just that you are really asking for it if you go around boasting.

I like to think of myself as a modern, rational human being but I still feel a slight sense of horror when I see someone put a pair of shoes on a table, even though I'm pretty sure that disaster really doesn't befall everyone who does. Actually I think I might be a bit like the old fellow who when asked if he believed in Fairies replied, "No, but they're there!"

- It is bad luck for a dog to run between a woman's legs.

- Many consider it a good omen if a dog eats grass.

- If a dog chases its tail, a ship will sink.

SOMETHING TO CROW ABOUT

These black birds may have something important to tell you.

The old saying goes:

> *One crow sorrow*
> *Two crows joy*
> *Three crows letter (or girl)*
> *Four crows a boy*
> *Five crows silver*
> *Six crows gold*
> *Seven crows a secret, yet to be told.*
> *Eight crows for a wish.*
> *Nine crows for a kiss.*
> *Ten crows for a time of joyous bliss.*

- Seeing one crow is believed to be bad luck. If you spit when you see that crow, however, you'll fend off the bad luck. Another version suggests you can erase the bad luck by making the sign of a cross.

- It was believed by First Nations people that crows were sent to Earth to escort the souls of the recently deceased to meet their Creator.

- A single crow in a cemetery is a sign that there will be a funeral within the week.

- Two crows flying over a house foretell a birth in that household.

- It is bad luck to see a single crow at a wedding, but good luck to see a pair.

Peter Coade

Peter Coade is an original Maritimer. He was born and brought up in the north end of Halifax, the Hydrostone. His wife is also from Halifax. His weather forecasts for various broadcasters have made him a local celebrity. He currently works for CBC Halifax.

Well, for the life of me I can't seem to come up with any "original" maritime weather folklore. In doing some digging around, however, I have discovered some tried and true old ones.

"Little snow, big snow, big snow, little snow." One often hears this statement at the start of a snowfall — looking at the size of the flakes as they fall. My explanation for this would be that the larger flakes are falling from the type of cloud that produces flurries; a convective type of cloud (summertime showers) and in passing any one spot would not necessarily produce a great snowfall.

The reason the flakes are larger is because of the upward and downward motion of air within this type of cloud, is great enough to cause the flakes to join together. These flakes are held in suspension within the cloud until they are too large for these "updrafts" and they fall to earth. This is not to say that you will not get a lot of snow from "flurries" — lines of these sometimes develop and can produce snow squalls. But generally, these flurries come and go and are of shorter duration.

Now the smaller flakes would then come from the type of cloud that does not have as great or as many updrafts and

If crows fly low, winds going to blow.
If crows fly high, winds going to die.
When sea birds fly to land there truly is a storm at hand.

downdrafts and therefore can fall as the water vapor develops them into snowflakes.

How about an explanation of "red sky at night, sailors delight; red sky in the morning, sailors take warning." This saying can be found in Shakespeare and also in the Bible in slightly different forms, but in climatology it comes from the fact that in the northern hemisphere weather systems typically move from west to east.

If the sky is red at night (sunset) then what is producing the redness (dust, impurities in the atmosphere) is to the west. It will be an area of stable air, usually denoted by high pressure, which is a "fair-weather" producer. Therefore, that area of stable air, fair weather, will be moving towards you. If however the red sky is in the morning — the east — then the fair weather area of high pressure has passed by and is now to the east.

And one more oldie but goody: "Cold enough to freeze the balls of a brass monkey." I actually did once explain this to a radio audience. Back in the days of wooden ships and iron men, cannon balls were made of iron. They sat in a cradle beside the gun. This cradle was made of brass and had indentations in it to hold the iron balls. It was called a "monkey." Because iron and brass have different qualities, they will contract (or expand) at different rates at different temperatures. In cold temperatures, the brass contracts at a greater rate than the iron, so the balls would have a tendency to fall off the monkeys.

Chapter 2

As Time Goes By

According to my grandmother, the best day of the week to be born is Sunday. Wednesday was the worst day of the week to come into the world, as bad luck would follow you for your entire life.

I remember asking her once why she thought this was so. As often was the case, she couldn't offer any credible explanation, except that she had "heard" that it was so.

Even though she couldn't explain the origins of most of her superstitions, my grandmother remained adamant that her beliefs were gospel. The generations of women before her had imparted their wisdom to anyone who would listen. If you didn't pay attention, you did so at your own peril.

Such superstitions offered an explanation about the world around them. In many cases, these beliefs were tied closely to the natural cycle of the seasons along with the rotation of the planets and the orbit of the moon. My grandfather, who maintained a large garden on his farm in Buckfield in Queens County, Nova Scotia, vehemently believed that the moon could predict when tragedy would befall family and friends. The moon was so revered as an oracle that farmers would trust it to tell them when the best time was to plant and harvest crops.

Indeed my grandfather planned his planting schedule around the cycle of the moon. I suspect most farmers from his generation and those before him acted in similar fashion. He believed that crops planted on the 31st of any month would not grow. In fact, so ingrained were his beliefs that he would not plant so much as one seed on the last day of any month, whether that month had 31 days or not.

What better example of superstitions revolving around time than the belief that if the 13th day of a month falls on a Friday, it is a day filled with bad luck. The Stress Management Center and Phobia Institute in Asheville, North Carolina, estimates that 17 to 21 million people in the United States alone are affected by a fear of this day. In fact, some people are so paralyzed by fear that they avoid their normal routines of doing business, taking flights, or even getting out of bed.

THE DREADED 13

The belief that bad luck will prevail on Friday the 13th is the most widely held superstition in the world. It is both feared and celebrated around the globe. It has been shunned and embraced throughout history by many cultures. Some historians believe that this fear in Christians could have something to do with the fact that the Crucifixion took place on a Friday and that were 13 disciples at the Last Supper. People afflicted with a morbid, irrational fear of Friday the 13th are said to suffer from Paraskevidekatriaphobics

SHOOT THE MOON

The full moon is tied to many local superstitions, but did you know that each full moon of every month has its own name?

JANUARY: Wolf Moon or Old Moon as the New Year begins.

FEBRUARY: Snow Moon or Hunger Moon. The snow is typically heavier this time of year and hunting is more difficult.

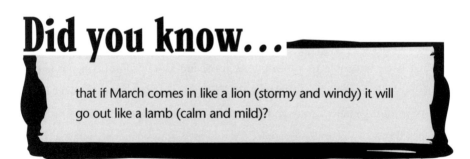

Did you know...

that if March comes in like a lion (stormy and windy) it will go out like a lamb (calm and mild)?

MARCH: Worm Moon as the frost begins to leave the ground and the worms begin to appear. Also known as the Sap Moon as the maple sap begins to flow.

APRIL: Pink Moon, Egg Moon or Fish Moon. With the arrival of spring, the fish are starting to run in the rivers and lakes.

MAY: Flower Moon or Planting Moon . This was the month when the gardens sprung to life.

JUNE: Strawberry Moon, Rose Moon or Hot Moon. The time of the summer solstice.

JULY: Buck Moon as the bucks begin to grow new antlers, or Thunder Moon.

AUGUST: Sturgeon Moon. It is said that more sturgeon are caught in the Great Lakes during this full moon than at any other time of the year. Also known as Grain Moon.

SEPTEMBER: Corn Moon because of the corn harvest. Also known as Barley Moon.

OCTOBER: Harvest Moon. This is when the full moon is nearest the fall equinox.

NOVEMER: Beaver Moon. Traditionally the time of year when beaver traps were set before the waterways froze. Also known as Frost Moon.

DECEMBER: Cold Moon or Long Nights Moon as this is when winter begins.

LOOK BEFORE YOU LEAP

Leap Year is not just another ordinary year.

The following is an old familiar Atlantic Canadian saying:

> *Thirty days hath September, April, June and November;*
> *All the rest have thirty-one,*
> *Excepting February alone*
> *Which hath but twenty-eight, in fine,*
> *Till leap year gives it twenty-nine.*

- February 29 occurs every four years and is said to be lucky and anything started on that day will be successful.

- Babies born on February 29 are said to be lucky and will go on to lead successful lives.

- Babies born on February 29 are said to be extremely healthy and will live long lives.

- It is also said that February 29 is the only time of the year when it is permitted for a woman to propose marriage to a man. It is bad luck for the man to say no.

- Some people believe the marriage will fail if it is held on February 29.

- As a weather predictor, if the sky is clear and bright on February 29, the next 12 months will be filled with storms.

SEVEN DAYS A WEEK

Does the day of the week you were born really determine your future?

Superstitious people will tell you that the day of the week on which you are born will determine the kind of person you are.

SUNDAY:
You tend to be optimistic and positive.
Good luck tends to follow you.
You should wear gold to improve your fortune.

MONDAY:
You tend to have an active imagination.
Generally, people like to be around you.
Silver is your good luck charm.

TUESDAY:
If you are born on this date, red is your colour.
You tend to be enthusiastic about life.
You have an ability to influence others.

WEDNESDAY:
Blue brings you good luck.
You tend to get along well with other people.
You do not like to argue.

THURSDAY:
You love to travel and discover new places.
You tend to be carefree.
The sign of the cross will bring you good luck.

FRIDAY:
You tend to fall in love easily.
Success will follow you throughout your life.
Diamonds will bring you good luck.

SATURDAY:
You are not afraid of hard work.
You tend to be more content with your life.
Like those born on Sunday, gold will also bring you good luck.

FULL OF GRACE

Monday's child is fair of face
Tuesday's child is full of grace
Wednesday's child is full of woe
Thursday's child has far to go
Friday's child is loving and giving
Saturday's child works hard for a living
But the child born on the Sabbath, is lucky, bonny, wise and gay.

THE DAWN OF A NEW DAY

Here's something to think about when planning your next New Year celebration.

- How you start the year is how you will end it, so you must ensure that you are wearing new clothes and looking your best, cleaned your house from top to bottom and have paid off all your debts. You should be with your partner to ensure that you are still with him/her at the next New Year.

- The first person you kiss after midnight on New Year's Eve will be true to you for the next 12 months.

- To ensure that you will have food throughout the coming year, make sure your cupboards are not empty when the New Year arrives.

Did you know...

that the Romans were the first to designate February 29 as Leap Year and that anyone born on February 29 can celebrate their birthday either on February 28 or March 1. Legally their birthday comes only every four years?

- It is bad luck for anything to leave your house, not even the garbage, during the first day of the New Year.

- If you do laundry on the first day of the New Year then it is said you are washing away the life of someone in your household and there will surely be a death in your home within the next 12 months.

- Do not lend or borrow on New Year's Day as you will be broke for the remainder of the year.

- If you cry on the first day of the New Year, then it is said you will shed many tears throughout the year.

- To break something made of glass on New Year's Day means your heart will break by the end of the New Year.

- If the wind is calm and the weather is fine on New Year's Day then there will be no major storms during the coming year.

Did you know...

that a spell of unusually warm weather in the first week of August means that there will be a white winter. And if there is a cold winter a hot summer will follow?

Allan Lynch

Allan Lynch is a Nova Scotia based travel writer and author who, happy to have survived his childhood, no longer complains about his health. Lynch is the author of the Nova Scotia Book of Musts and other titles. He has written for magazines and journals around world for more than three decades.

I joke with doctors that I don't know why they bother with medical school when all you have to do is go to a Tim Horton's. No matter what your medical condition, Tim's patrons have either had it or know someone who has had it, and will proceed to prescribe the proper treatment.

When I was growing up we didn't have Tim's, but I had a lot of home remedies administered by my parents, aunts and grandparents. Uncles seemed to know of the treatments, but were exempted from doctoring.

As a kid whenever I got an earache my father would blow smoke in my ear. Nowadays, that would get you charged with child abuse, but it always seemed to work. I don't know if there was something to it or just the placebo effect of having someone pay attention to you, sort of like when your mom kissed a hurt.

Chest colds were always treated with a heavy slathering of goose grease. It sounds so Dickensian but when I was growing up my parents would always get a goose and a capon for Christmas. We would take it down to the Kentville Pastry Shop, they would cook them in their ovens, and we would pick up the birds on Christmas Eve. The Christmas goose always supplied the grease needed for chest treatments. It was rubbed all over my chest and then a piece of flannel about the size of a diaper would be cut from a sheet and laid over the grease. Then I would put on a T-shirt under my pajamas and go to bed.

I've always had eye problems and as a kid (gawd I sound sickly). I used to get a lot of sties. It always infuriated me when someone would say urinating on the side of the road caused a sty. I lived in town where people didn't urinate on the roadside. There really wasn't much of a treatment for a sty. A hot water bottle was about the best anyone did, sometimes a patch, but never black like a pirate like the one I wanted.

One of the popular warnings we got as kids was not to sit on the ground before June 1st. If we sat on the cold ground before then we were sure to get rickets or polio. I think this old wives' tale was mostly made up by mothers to try to keep us from getting our clothes dirty.

The most diabolical treatment in the family medicine chest was the mustard poultice. Have a boil or a sore back? Someone was sure to mix up a mustard poultice for you. I don't know what the ingredients were, but I do remember screams as it was applied.

I remember that the mustard mixture would be slathered on bread, which was then securely taped over the painful area so you got the extra jolt of pain when the heavy tape was ripped off. However the poultice may have hurt, it was preferable to the flesh-lifting pain you got from the ancient bottle of Minard's Liniment my grandfather Lynch kept in the back of his pantry.

He used this liniment on horses and people. The family always joked that Grampy felt that if it was good enough for livestock it was good enough for us. The moment you saw him reaching for that shelf, you suddenly found yourself cured.

Joel Plaskett

Joel Plaskett has been a prominent figure in the Canadian indie rock scene of the 1990s and 2000s. He was played to sold-out clubs and theatres throughout Canada, the U.S., U.K., and Australia. He has won countless ECMA awards and earned several Juno nominations (including Songwriter of the Year along side Neil Young), and was the First Place Winner in the 2008 Great American Song Contest and the Billboard World Song Contest, for "Fashionable People" (in the Pop Category).

I don't necessarily consider myself to be a particularly superstitious person, but, hey, I don't walk under a ladder. On second thought, I guess I do harbour a few superstitions after all. Like when somebody opens an umbrella inside I'm like, hey, what are you doing? That's bad luck, man. Don't do that.

As far as superstitions in the entertainment world, I'm not sure if the things we do would be considered superstitions or if they would be classified as being practical. Maybe they're like a ritual. For example, you hear this one a lot: bad sound check, great show. I've experienced it myself many times. If you go to sound check and nothing sounds right and everyone's in a bad mood, then when you take the stage that night, you turn out having a great show. That's one thing I heard a lot about and you know, based on what I've seen, I think that's a fairly accurate superstition.

STARTING THE NEW YEAR RIGHT

With a little good luck to carry you through.

- In some homes, on New Year's Eve, dishes of fresh fruit are set out as an "offering" and as a means to invite good luck into the home throughout the year.

- It is good luck to eat cabbage for dinner on the first day of the New Year.

- Babies born on January 1 will always have good luck.

- It is good luck to dance around a tree on New Year's Day.

- It is good luck to wear a new piece of clothing on the first day of the New Year.

Chapter 3

Body Language

If our bodies could talk, what exactly would they say? The answer to that question for me is as varied as the personalities in my family. According to my parents, grandparents, and other relatives, your body could tell you lots of things, but you have to pay attention and recognize and interpret the signs. There are, of course, many superstitions surrounding the body, and as a youngster growing up in rural Nova Scotia I heard many of them.

If your right palm itches, you're going to shake hands with a stranger. If it's the palm of your left hand, you're going to come into some money. The catch here, according to my father, was that in order for your good fortune to materialize, you had to spit into your left palm and then rub it on your left buttock. Does it work? You be the judge. I've tried it many times and I'm still waiting for my ship to come in.

It doesn't stop with the hands. Other body parts hold certain powers. If the bottoms of your feet itch it means you're soon going to walk over strange land. A ringing in your ears? Someone is saying bad things about you. An itchy nose? Someone is thinking about you or it might also mean that you are going to kiss a fool, meet a stranger, or get in a fight.

But of all the superstitions I've heard about body language, this is the most unnerving. If you get a sudden chill, someone just walked on your grave.

It is difficult to pinpoint exactly where these beliefs originated. It is possible, however, that an old aunt of mine held the key to their evolution. Whenever my aunt complained that the little toe on her right foot ached, we'd usually have bad weather. Mere coincidence?

Perhaps. But it has been a long held belief that people with arthritic bones may experience aches and pains just prior to a storm. It is likely then, that much like this belief evolved, so too have other superstitions.

DRESSED FOR . . .

What you wear can say a lot about you and what kind of day you may have.

- Missing a button hole while buttoning up your shirt is considered bad luck.

- Wearing odd socks is bad luck.

- It is bad luck to wear a hat while sitting at the dinner table.

- It is said to be bad luck to wear anything white after Labor Day.

- If you drop a glove, it is unlucky for you to pick it up. You should ask someone else to get it for you.

- It is unlucky to get dressed by putting on your shirt with the left arm first. This left first holds true for pants and shoes. Always start with the right side of your body to ensure that you have a good day.

- Always button your shirt from the neck down.

- Putting your shirt on inside out is bad luck, but if you change your shirt, you can change your luck.

- It is said to be good luck if you put your sweater on inside out, but you must wear it all day for the charm to work.

- When you put on new clothes for the first time, you should make a wish.

Did you know...
that it is bad luck to sneeze to the left?

GESUNDHEIT

The way you sneeze can say a lot about what kind of person you are.

If you . . .

Sneeze on Monday, you sneeze for danger.

Sneeze on Tuesday, you will kiss a stranger.

Sneeze on Wednesday, you sneeze for a letter.

Sneeze on Thursday, you sneeze for the better.

Sneeze on Friday, you sneeze for sorrow.

Sneeze on Saturday, you will see your beau tomorrow.

Sneeze on Sunday and bad luck will follow you all week.

- Place a hand in front of your mouth when sneezing. Your soul may escape otherwise.

- When someone sneezes you should say "God Bless You", because at one time it was believed that the Devil entered your mouth when you opened it to sneeze.

- This is much the same reasoning behind why some people will say "God Bless Me" when they sneeze. However, there is real meaning to this old saying. At one time in some cultures it was considered a sin to sneeze.

- Looking directly at the sun will cause you to sneeze.

THE NUMBER OF TIMES YOU SNEEZE IN A ROW HAS MEANING

Sneeze once for sorrow.

Sneeze twice for joy.

Sneeze three times for a letter.

Sneeze four times for a boy.

Sneeze five times for silver.

Sneeze six times for gold.

Sneeze seven times for a secret that will never to be told.

THE EYES HAVE IT

Ever wonder what your eyes would say if they could talk?

- If you find a loose eyelash, you should place it on the back of your hand and lightly blow it off. While doing so, you should make a wish.

- It was once thought that people whose eyebrows had grown together were evil.

- If your eyelid twitches, it was believed that you are going to soon hear about a tragic death.

- People with two different colored eyes were once said to be witches.

WALK A MILE IN THESE SHOES

These superstitions have a lot of sole.

- Never give shoes for Christmas gifts as it will cause your friend to walk away.

- It is bad luck to wear new shoes on Christmas Day.

- It is bad luck to leave your shoes upside down with the soles facing up.

- If you accidentally see footwear turned over, such as shoes or slippers, you will quarrel with someone close to you.

- Never wear new shoes to a funeral, as the souls of the deceased will get angry and haunt you.

- If you tie someone's shoelaces, make a wish as you're doing so.

- If your shoe lace comes undone that means you are about to take a trip. However, you should be cautious as it could mean you might encounter bad luck on that trip.

Rita MacNeil

Rita MacNeil, a native of Big Pond, Cape Breton, first performed on stage in 1971 and recorded her first album, "Born a Woman," in 1975. She performed at folk festivals throughout the 1970s and 1980s, culminating in her major label debut and pop break-through in 1987. Her biggest hit, "Flying On Your Own," was a crossover Top 40 hit in 1987. In 1990, MacNeil was the bestselling country artist in Canada, outselling Garth Brooks. Rita hosted a CBC Television variety show, "Rita and Friends," from 1994 to 1997. She runs a tea room in her hometown which has become one of Cape Breton Island's most popular tourist attractions. She was made a Member of the Order of Canada in 1992. She was awarded the Order of Nova Scotia in 2005.

I'm not sure I necessarily consider myself to be a very superstitious person, but coming from Cape Breton I've heard many of them. When you hear these things when you're a youngster, they sort of scare you, but when you're older you question the origins behind them. That, for me, is the most interesting part about superstitions.

One of the most common superstitions I remember from my childhood is the one that says if you put on a sweater inside out you weren't to change it or your whole day would go awry. Do I believe it? Let's just say I've never been known to change one of my sweaters.

Another one I recall is the superstition that says if you bought a new pair of shoes, you should never, ever, put them on the table or that would bring you a full year of bad luck. You might laugh at that, but I find that even today, as an adult, when I buy a new pair of shoes and put them on the table, even if they are still in the bag, I wonder if I should really do that.

As for other superstitions, I'm not sure if I really follow any. I do, however, have several rituals I do before I go on stage, including rocking back and forth. And I always make sure that I am back stage 15 minutes before I go on. Maybe it's just a habit, but it's something I always do. I guess that's kind of a superstition.

Denyse Sibley

Denyse Sibley was born to a farming family and was raised in Nova Scotia's Musquodoboit Valley. She is a radio host of FX Country Breakfast on CHFX-FM FX 101.9 in Halifax. She has four children.

You have to wonder why, with all the scientific data available to us today, so many of us still cling to beliefs passed down from generation to generation. When Vernon first asked me to do this, I was privately thinking "How hard can this be?" because I am NOT superstitious. That was then.

Leave it to my mother! After talking with her and comparing notes, I'm thinking how much I will have to eat my words. There are so many things that I do or don't do based on how I've been raised and what I've been told.

How many times have you been told growing up, that if you blow out all the candles on your birthday cake with the first puff you will get your wish? How ridiculous, right, but I have told my own kids that soooo many times. Hmmm. So here are some others I like:

- Feed a cold and starve a fever.

- Big snow/little snow. Little snow/big snow.

- You'll catch cold walking with wet hair.

- Don't crack your knuckles; it causes arthritis and enlarged joints.

- Step on a spider AND it will rain.

- See a falling star . . . close your eyes and make a wish.

- Never talk about a bad dream before breakfast because it may become reality.

- Knock on wood.

- Need a cold winter to kill bugs. Heard this over and over again growing up. Funny, though, there are still lots of bugs come summer. I have a tough time with that one.

AND I had hoped this to be true....

Eat an egg with double or multiple yolks if you want to give birth to twins. Why, I even crossed my fingers and wished upon a falling star. Growing up on a farm I had the opportunity to eat many farm fresh eggs - "Double yolkers". I did have four beautiful healthy babies, but no twins.

Ask me if I'm superstitious and I'd probably say, "No not me. Are you kidding?" However, I will not open an umbrella indoors. Isn't there some sort of scientific research to support that one?

WANT A SHOE SIGN?

These tips may put a shine to your day.

- It is considered good luck if you break a lace while trying to tie your shoe.

- It is good luck to tie your old shoes together and then hang them from a nail.

- Burning an old pair of shoes on Christmas Eve is said to bring you good luck.

- If your new shoes squeak when you walk it means that you haven't paid for them yet, but if your old shoes squeak it is considered good luck.

- Holes in the bottom your shoes are a sign you're going to get some money.

Did you know...

that unmarried girls may throw a shoe over their shoulders at the door. If the shoe lands with its toe pointing towards the door, then the girl will marry within a year. If not, the girl will have to wait at least another year?

LET ME HEAR YOUR BODY TALK

These signs may be subtle, but perhaps you should listen.

- Never have a hair cut in March or you will have a headache for the remainder of the year.

- If your left ear itches, it is said that someone is saying something bad about you. Conversely, if the right ear itches, then it is believed that someone is saying something good about you.

- If your feet ache, it is going to rain.

- If the bottom of your feet itch, you are going to walk on the ground where you will someday be buried.

- By making the sign of the Christian faith with our fingers, you drive away evil spirits.

- If you bite your tongue, someone is talking badly about you. Bite your sleeve to make them stop. It can also mean you are going to kiss a fool.

- If you pull out a grey or white hair will 10 more will grow in its place.

Did you know...

that people with hiccups were once thought to be possessed by the devil?

Chapter 4

Brides and Babes

Centuries ago when men literally "captured" a woman for marriage or when a couple wanted to marry but the bride's family took issue with the union, the groom's best swordsman stood guard during the ceremony. It was his job to defend the couple and keep the family at bay until the couple could escape.

In some instances, the best man accompanied the groom to capture a potential bride from a neighboring village. This forceful taking of a woman was the reason she stood on the left, leaving the groom's fighting arm free to fend off attackers.

No single event or activity in our modern society has more traditions and superstitions attached to it than marriage. We've heard them all. It's bad luck for the groom to see the bride on the wedding day prior to the ceremony. If the groom drops the wedding ring during the ceremony, the marriage is doomed to failure. It is bad luck for anyone else other than the bride to wear white on the wedding day. There are many variations of these modern superstitions, but most have their roots firmly planted in the past.

In ancient times the wedding band was used as partial payment for a bride. It also indicated a pledge to marry. The ring was worn on the third finger of the right hand because it was believed the vein in this finger traveled directly to the heart.

In earlier generations, daughters were considered their father's property. If the father agreed with the marriage, he escorted his property down the isle and transferred ownership to the groom. That would explain today's practice of a father (or his stand-in) "giving away" his daughter to the groom.

Even the first kiss had deeper meaning than simply being a display of love between the bride and groom. In fact, centuries ago, there was little romance attached to the first kiss. In truth, the act was meant to seal the contract between the couple, a practice that dates back to early Roman times. If the couple did not kiss, the marriage was not legal.

And if you think that carrying the bride over the threshold was a gesture of love and good luck, think again. In ancient times, when a bride was forcefully taken, she was often unwilling to enter the marriage chambers. The groom dragged or carried her across the threshold. Another belief surrounding this custom is that when a bride first entered the home, evil spirits could be carried in on her feet. If she was carried, these spirits became confused and could not enter the home.

But superstitions surrounding love, marriage and having babies, don't stop here. There are, literally, dozens more. Here are some of them.

ALWAYS A BRIDESMAID . . .

Not all marriages are made in heaven.

- If you cannot make a good fire, you will not get a good husband.

- Burn a match to the end, and it will make the initial of the first name of the man you are to marry.

- When going into a vacant house, throw a ball of yarn and say, "I pull, who winds?" The one you are to marry will answer you.

- Try this on Halloween. If you can eat an apple that is suspended on a string from the ceiling, you will marry within the year.

Did you know...

that although many couples tie the knot on the weekend, traditionally Wednesday was the day which promised matrimonial bliss. It was once considered bad luck to marry on Saturday?

- The number of candles left on the birthday cake after you blow once, will be the number of years until you are married.

- Hang a wishbone over the front door and the first man who passes under it is the man you will marry.

- If two forks are at a place setting on a table, the one who sits there will get married.

- Hold the bride's dress on your lap for ten minutes, and you will be a bride within the year.

- If a bride wears another girl's garter when she is married, that girl will be married within the year.

- The number of nails in the horseshoe when you pick it up, will be the number of years until you are married.

- If a black cat takes up its home at a house, the unmarried daughters will have a good chance to marry.

- If a woman sees a robin flying overhead on Valentine's Day, it meant she will marry a sailor. If she sees a sparrow, she will marry a poor man and be very happy. If she sees a goldfinch, she will marry a rich man.

- Any bridesmaid that carries a piece of the wedding cake in her pocket until the bride and groom's honeymoon is over will marry very soon.

. . . NEVER A BRIDE

- If you take the last piece of bread off the plate when it is not offered, you will never be married.

- If you look at the moon through a knothole, you will never be married.

- If you take the last piece of anything, you will be an old maid unless you kiss the cook.

- If the bridesmaid is older than the bride, she should wear something green, or else she may never marry.

- If you fall upstairs, you will not be married within the year.

- If you sweep a circle around a girl, she will never marry.

- Eat the point of a pie first and you will remain an old maid.

- If you look under the bed, you will not marry for another year.

Fact and Fiction

FICTION: It was once believed that if a woman was carrying her baby up high in the womb, the baby was a girl, whereas a boy was carried low. It was believed that girls needed more protection so the mother carried them higher in the womb than the boys

FACT: There is no scientific or medical research to support this.

WATER PROPHECY

A little H2O can say a lot.

- Go fishing on the first day of May. If you get a bite, it means you will soon meet your beau. If you get a catch, it means you will get a husband within the year.

- If you splash water on yourself while washing clothes, you will get a drunken husband.

- If a kettle of hot water is poured over the doorstep that the bride crosses, there will be another wedding in that house within the year.

- Look in a well on the first day of May and you will see the face of your future husband.

Dave Gunning

Dave Gunning, a singer/storyteller, grew up in Lyons Brook, Nova Scotia. He made his recording debut with "Lost Tracks" (1996), followed by "Caught Between Shadows" (2000), "Dave Gunning Live" (2002), "Two-Bit World" (2004) and "Dave Gunning Christmas" (2006). In September 2009 he released his seventh album entitled, "We're All Leaving." His ability to tell a story in his songs has resulted in six Music Nova Scotia awards and three East Coast Music Awards.

Well, as far as being superstitious goes, I wouldn't say that I consider myself to be overly concerned with that stuff, but I do make it a habit to always make sure that I have three guitar picks in my back pocket before I go stage. I've been doing that for as long as I can remember. Does that count?

Come to think of it, maybe I am superstitious after all.

HERE COMES THE BRIDE

Something old, something new, something borrowed, something blue … and a silver sixpence in your shoe.

Married on Monday,
married health.
Married on Sunday,
married for wealth.
Marry in lent; you'll live to repent

- It is considered bad luck to be married on a Friday in the month of May.

- June brides are said to be more fertile.

- Should a bride or groom encounter an open grave on their way to the chapel for their wedding, it is considered a foreboding sign of something terrible in their future.

- A bride should always wear a veil to protect her from evil.

- It is a good sign to see a rainbow on the day of your wedding.

- It is good luck for a cat to sneeze near the bride on her wedding day.

- Put the letters of the alphabet in a pan of water under your bed. The next morning the letter of your future husband will be turned over.

- If a young bride bites into an apple and finds a worm, it means she will be blessed with lots of babies.

- The first gift the bride opens should be the first gift she uses.

- Having the bride and groom jump over a broom handle would ensure them having a long, happy life together.

- If a bride drops a pair of scissors while working on her wedding gown, it means her fiancée has been unfaithful.

- A bride and groom should never be married on either birthday. It is bad luck.

- June, October and December are the luckiest months for a wedding.

- Marry in June and your husband will treat you well.

- If a bride breaks her wedding ring it means she will soon be a widow.

- If the wedding ring is lost, the couple will soon separate.

- It is good luck for the bride to find a spider in her wedding gown.

- If it rains on your wedding day, it is a sign that you will shed many tears during your married life.

- In Cape Breton, brides hang a rosary on the clothes line the night before the wedding to ensure good weather. Some believe rain on your wedding day means you will have many children.

- It is bad luck to postpone a wedding.

- To awaken the bride on her wedding morning is bad luck. Let her sleep as long as she will.

- If anyone should see the bride's veil before the wedding, her married life will be unhappy.

- As long as you keep some of the bread of your first wedded meal, you will never be in want.

- It is held that a final look in the mirror right before the bride leaves her home for the ceremony will bring good luck. However, if she looks in a mirror once again before the ceremony, her luck will tarnish to bad!

Diane Lynn Tibert

Diane Lynn Tibert grew up carefree with her spirited parents and nine siblings in a tidy home at Cole Harbour. She has been a freelance writer since 1999 and is the author of Roots to the Past *and writes a genealogy column published in several news-papers across Atlantic Canada. When she isn't chasing fairies through cemeteries, sketching dwarfs and writing her fantasy novel, she can be found camping with her three children and exploring the rest of the province.*

Growing up with parents born before 1930 meant our lives were intertwined with superstition. My father was born in rural Nova Scotia to German and Scottish parents and as a result was influenced by the many traditions and folklore passed down through the generations. My mother, born and raised in Newfoundland, was swayed by the whims of Irish and Scottish legends and lore. When she settled in Nova Scotia in 1945, she brought the quaint and sometimes quirky superstitions with her.

Under no circumstances was an umbrella opened in our house because bad luck would escape its confines and haunt the home. Worse still was if the person put the open umbrella over their head while inside; bad luck would rain down upon them. To this day, my mother and many family members follow this rule. Much to her dismay, from an early age, I have tried to disprove this superstition with the deliberate opening and flaunting of umbrellas inside the home.

As children do, I often ran in one door and out the other. But this was frowned upon in our home. We were told we had dropped our good luck at the entry threshold and by going out another door we went outside without protection. To this day, I still think about going out the same door I entered to maintain my good luck.

Early in life, we didn't have blinds in the windows. When they were installed in the kitchen, it began a whole new superstition. If a blind suddenly went up without assistance, it was said that somebody we knew died. I once asked my mother what happened if the entire blind fell to the floor. She said, "It was time to buy a new blind."

Many times while driving with my parents, if they saw a couple walking hand-in-hand together alongside the road, they commented about the woman's position. If she were on the inside, away from the road, she was a keeper and the man looked at no other woman. If she walked nearer the road, closer to the vehicles, it indicated the man was making her available to other men and that he was not committed to the relationship.

LET THEM EAT CAKE . . .

Or maybe not.

- It is bad luck for a bride to bake her own wedding cake.

- If a bride tastes the wedding cake before it is cut, she will lose her husband's love.

- If a bride saves a piece of her wedding cake, she ensures that her husband will be forever faithful.

- The top layer of the wedding cake should be frozen and thawed on the first anniversary to rekindle their romance, or it is served at the christening of their first child.

PLAYING FOOTSIE . . .

With the wedding plans.

- To ensure a long and happy marriage, when getting dressed for the wedding, the bride should always put her right shoe on first.

- The bride should also step into the church with her right foot first.

Did you know...

that veils were once used to mask the identity of the woman until the ceremony was complete. If another man was in love with the bride, he wouldn't be able to kidnap her for himself. Some cultures used the veil to hide the bride's face to ward off bad luck?

- If the bride burns a pair of her old shoes the night before the wedding, it will not rain on her wedding day.

- If a bride puts on her left shoe first, her married life will be unhappy.

- It is bad luck for a bride to put her bare feet on the floor on the night of the wedding.

- If a woman tears her wedding shoes, she will be beaten by her husband.

- A week before the wedding, it is considered good luck to have a cat eat out of your left shoe.

THE BABY BLUES

We're not talking baby talk here.

- If you dream of death, then a baby will come into the family.

- If a woman suffers from heartburn while she is pregnant, the baby will have a full head of hair.

- It is good luck to kiss a baby on the forehead.

- If you rub money on a baby's head, he or she will be rich in the future.

- Placing a bible under you baby's pillow will keep away evil spirits.

- If you step over a child, that child will remain short.

- To cure a baby's hiccups give him or her a mixture of water and sugar.

- Never tickle the bottom of baby's feet because it will make him or her stutter when the get older.

- It is bad luck to let a baby look at itself in a mirror before it is a year old.

- Keep cats away from babies because they "suck the breath" of the child.

PREGNANCY PREDICTIONS

Boy or Girl? These tidbits may tell.

- It is considered bad luck for a pregnant woman to cross her legs.

- It is believed that if a pregnant woman suffers from back pain, she will give birth to a boy.

- It is believed that if a woman is burned during her pregnancy her baby will be born with a birthmark in the exact location as the burn.

- It is said that if a pregnant woman carries her baby high, she will have a boy. Conversely, if she carries the baby low, it will be a girl.

ACCORDING TO LEGEND

To predict the sex of a baby, take a pin, needle or wedding ring and attach it to a thread or strand of hair. Hold the dangling item over the pregnant woman's belly while she is lying down. If the needle or wedding ring swings in a strong circular motion, she will have a girl. If it moves and swings like a pendulum, the baby is a boy.

Did you know...

that seeing a grey horse on the way to a church is considered lucky for the bride and groom?

WHAT A WOMAN WANTS

Strange superstitions make for an empty jewelery box.

- Opal is the birthstone for anyone born in October. It is bad luck for anyone other than people born in October to wear an opal.

- It is bad luck for a husband and wife to give each other a watch as it's a sign they will soon break up.

- A man should never gift his fiancé with a new pair of shoes or she will walk away from him.

A CLEAN SWEEP . . . FOR LUCK

It is interesting to note that people can be seen as being omens as well. For instance, there was once a tradition of making sure that a chimney sweep met the bridal couple on their wedding day. Seeing a chimney sweep meant their good luck would last throughout the year.

AND SO IT IS SAID:

Two lovers will never agree after their marriage if both wipe their faces on the same towel.

WHAT'S THAT, HONEY?

The honeymoon tradition is rooted in the past when the groom captured a bride. The couple hid while the moon passed through its phases. During this time, it was hoped the woman would become pregnant, in which case her family would want her to remain with her husband. To encourage fertility and to increase the chance of a male child, the couple drank honey wine or mead.

Chapter 5

Creepy Crawlers

We've all heard the old superstition that if you stomp on a spider, you'll cause it to rain the next day. While difficult to pinpoint the exact origins of this age-old belief, it is most likely that this superstition stemmed from someone's fear of spiders.

My theory is that in an effort to avoid the eight-legged creepy crawler someone somewhere warned that if you killed a spider it would rain. This myth may be easy to dispel by stomping on a spider. Whatever reason may be, this warning has endured and has survived the test of time.

Arachnophobes feel more than just uneasy in any area they believe could harbor spiders or that has visible signs of their presence. They are literally unable to enter the general vicinity until they have overcome the panic attack associated with their phobia. In some extreme cases, even a picture or a realistic drawing of a spider can trigger fear.

While spiders play a prominent role in many long-held superstitions, they are certainly not the only creepy crawlers or winged creatures to be scorned and feared. Mosquitoes, for example, have been the bane of our existence for centuries and there are many "tried and true" methods of battling this pesky summertime bloodsucker.

And speaking of bloodsuckers, what creepy things are more hated and loathed than wood ticks? Many myths surround these disease carrying cling-ons. But not all things bug-related are bad luck. For example, it is said that discovering a lady-bug in your home will bring you good luck or if a grasshopper jumps on you good fortune will soon follow.

It's funny how much these superstitions control our lives. I have vivid memories from my childhood of being told by my elders that I should never kill a spider because I'd cause it to rain. Even to this day when I see a spider scoot across the floor, those earlier warnings come rushing back to me and I'm reminded that is exactly how these beliefs survive the passage of time.

BUG OFF

Do creepy crawlers bug you? Here's what you can do.

- Plant marigolds in your gardens. The bugs, especially mosquitoes, are said to hate their smell. Try planting them throughout your vegetable gardens or place pots of them on your deck and patio.

- Sage and Rosemary are good, natural bug repellants. Try keeping a few pots of these herbs around your outside spaces.

- Lavender works the same magic.

- Mint is also another good, natural plant that is said to keep away the flies.

- Slices of cucumber spread around your picnic blanket will keep the ants from invading.

- Lemon juice and cinnamon are also worth a try. But it's not for wearing. Try spreading it around your deck or wherever you're going to be.

- A mixture of soap and water is good for keeping earwigs under control as well as other pests that enjoy munching on your plants.

- Baking soda may be good for killing pet odors and other smells, but if you have fleas in your carpets, sprinkle sea salt on your floors and then quickly vacuum.

- Garlic is good for discouraging flies, mosquitoes and ants. Place it around your yard and house if you can tolerate the smell.

- Spreading crushed eggshells throughout your garden will keep away slugs and snails.

- Rubbing a slice of onion over an insect bite will stop itching and help prevent infection.

Did you know...

that it is bad luck to kill a ladybug as it represents the Virgin Mary?

MOSQUITO MISERY

A nice way to say buzz off!

- Burning cow manure will keep the mosquitoes at bay.

- People who wear hats or keep their heads covered are said to be bothered less by mosquitoes than those who do not.

- The clothes you wear may attract the little pests. Wearing light colored clothing may keep the mosquitoes from bothering you.

- Orange peelings are supposedly good at repelling mosquitoes.

- Eating garlic is also said to be a good way to keep the mosquitoes from biting.

- Smear yourself with baby oil to keep the mosquitoes from biting.

CRICKETS SPEAK

And we are not talking about the Disney character.

- It is good luck to find a cricket in your house.

- It is bad luck to kill a cricket.

- To hear cricket sing in the morning before sunrise is a sign of a stormy day.

- To hear crickets sing at night indicates a clear night.

- It is good luck if a cricket manages to get into your house and starts to chirp.

Did you know...

that seeing a spider run down its web in the middle of the afternoon means you are going to take a trip?

I DON'T LIKE SPIDERS AND SNAKES

These creepy crawlers can predict the future and tell you if your luck will be good or bad.

- If spiders build their webs high off the ground in the summer and fall, it means lots of snow in the winter.

- If you kill the first snake you see in the springtime, it is said you kill your worst enemy.

- A snake in your house? That is said to be bad luck.

- Finding a spider in a drinking glass is said to be bad luck or sickness

- Finding a spider in your kitchen sink is a sign that a tragedy is about to befall your household.

- A spider in your bed, means your marriage is in trouble.

- If you find a spider in your house in January, it means you should expect an early spring.

Did you know...

that smoke will keep mosquitoes at bay particularly if it's smoke from burning maple?

Fact and Fiction

FICTION: That a person who sees a Luna moth will eventually go mad.

FACT: People rarely see Luna moths, mostly because they fly late at night in spring and early summer. It is a treat to see one of these very beautiful insects. Adult Luna moths don't eat, they don't even have a mouths. They live for just a week, and their only purpose is to mate.

Peter Harrison

Peter Harrison is co-host of C100 FM's Breakfast Club, the top-rated radio station in Halifax.

I grew up in rural Nova Scotia. I tell people I'm from Parrsboro when I'm asked, but my mother corrects me if she's within earshot. Truth be told, I'm from Harrison Settlement, about 12 kilometers north of Parrsboro on the old highway to Amherst. I think I was one of the last people in the province to go to a one-room schoolhouse. When I was going to elementary school in the mid-60s, 18 kids attended Halfway River West from primary to Grade 6 and, yes, there was an outhouse out back to look after us when nature called.

Needless to say, we also had our share of superstitions . . . although I'm not sure if they were that much different from superstitions held in other parts of Atlantic Canada. One that sticks with me to this day is the litany of expressions that follows counting the number of crows you see at any one time, "one crow sorrow, two crow joy . . . ." There are, apparently, variations of this rhyme from around the English-speaking world. I cannot pass by a murder of crows without repeating the rhyme to see what fate awaits me. Nor can I pass a single crow without thinking or saying out loud, "God bless one black crow" to ward off the sorrow that would normally accompany one crow.

Again, these superstitions might be universal, but we certainly believed that if you dropped a fork a stranger would come knocking. If a bird flew in the house there would be a death, and bad things happen in threes.

"Sunday plans never stand." That's another old wives' tale that my mother was fond of. I think it was more of an excuse for not committing to something she really didn't want to do in the first place. When she was particularly frustrated with my two older brothers (or me), my mother would utter the phrase "Jesus wept." When pressed, she would tell us it was the shortest sentence in the bible and not really swearing.

By the way, the shortest sentence in the English language is "I am." A wise man once told me the longest sentence in the English language is "I do."

SPIDER IN THE MORNING

A spider in the morning is a sign of sorrow;

A spider at noon brings worry for tomorrow;

A spider in the afternoon is a sign of a gift;

But a spider in the evening will all hopes uplift.

Darrell Dexter

Darrell Dexter grew up in Milton, Queens County and trained as a lawyer. His political career began when he was elected to the city council of Dartmouth in 1994. He was first elected to the provincial House of Assembly in the 1998 and in 2001 he was elected leader of the Nova Scotia NDP. Dexter is married with one son. He led the NDP to the party's first ever election victory in June 2009.

When I think of growing up in Queens County, I think of all of the superstitions I heard and now they all seem so unremarkable. There were the usual augers of bad luck — broken mirrors, black cats, walking under ladders, etc.

I remember as a child I had some warts on my hand and my dad promptly took me out in the woods after a rain and found an old tree stump where water had collected. He had me wash the warts in the stump water. This was supposed to cure the warts and since I don't know what ever happened to them, I guess it worked.

TICKED OFF

What people know and what they think they know about ticks are two different things.

- Once attached to the body, they should never be pulled off because if their head or legs break off, they will infect and poison your body. *Not true.*

- Heat is the only effective method to make them detach from the body. *Not true.*

- The only way to kill a wood tick is to burn it. *Not true.*

- Wood ticks are so tough they cannot be crushed. *Not true.*

- Ticks can jump from one host to the next. *Not true.*

WHAT BUGS YOU?

And we're not talking about your pet peeves.

- It is rare to find a praying mantis, so if a woman finds one, it is considered to be very good luck. If a man finds one, it's a sign of his fertility and that he can father lots of children.

- If the first butterfly you see in the spring is white, it means you will have good luck for the remainder of the year.

- If a white moth tries to get into your house, it is a sign of death.

- It is good luck to see three butterflies in flight together.

- Finding a grasshopper in your house is good luck.

- Discovering a lady bug in your home is said to be good luck.

Chapter 6

From the Ground up

It should not come as a surprise that like just about everything else in this part of the world gardening has more than its fair share of superstitions. Many practices date back to a time when early civilizations worshiped gods and idols. They claim to see signs in nature that tell them when to plant and when to harvest, ensuring a rich bounty.

Have you heard that burning scraps of food around the base of fruit trees on the first day of spring will make them more fruitful come harvest time? Admittedly, I've never tried this, but over the years I've encountered many seasoned farmers who claim that the practice does produce noticeable results.

Maritime farmers and gardeners believe that planting potatoes during the full moon ensures a healthy harvest.

Early European civilizations believed that it was good luck to burn mushrooms, but bad luck if cattle were allowed to graze in a pasture where the mushrooms grew.

Some beliefs make perfectly good sense. In the Maritimes, it's a long-held belief that using rotting seaweed makes good fertilizer.

Fire has long been associated with land cleansing and the practice has continued throughout the ages. Perhaps the grass and under brush burning ritual each springtime, as is the habit in the Maritimes, may have originated with these early pagan burning rites. It kind of makes sense that this "burning" cleanses the land and makes way for fresh, virgin growth.

AN APPLE A DAY

Take a bite from this forbidden fruit and see what happens.

- Eat one apple a day, to be blessed with good health.

- If you cut an apple in half and count the seeds inside, that is the number of children you will have.

- You will have good health for the year, if you eat an apple at midnight on Christmas Eve.

- Think of three or four names of boys or girls you want to marry and then say them out loud as you are twisting the stem of an apple. Whatever name you are saying as the stem breaks off is the name of the person you are going to marry.

- It is bad luck to eat the seeds of an apple.

- If a woman eats an apple on Halloween, she will be married within a year.

- It is good luck to plant an apple core in your garden. It will fertilize your entire crop.

Did you know...

that apple growers believe it is good luck to eat the first apple of the fall harvest. It assures them good market prices.

EVERY BLOOMIN' THING

More than flowers grow in some gardens.

- It is said that if you imagine you can smell flowers, it is an omen of death.

- When you are giving flowers to someone who is ill, you should remember the superstitions attached to flower colours:

    White flowers are bad luck for any sick person.

    Red denotes blood and life and is good luck.

    Never give a bunch of red and white mixed together, especially to a hospital patient.

    Violet shows goodwill on the part of the giver.

    Yellow and orange, the colors of the sun, will brighten anyone's day.

- Never pick a flower from a grave and throw it away because it is said the place where it falls will become haunted and you'll have bad luck.

- Flowers planted during the new moon will bloom best.

- Sunflowers bring good luck to the entire garden.

Did you know...

that it is unlucky for a sick person to place flowers on their bed?

ACCORDING TO LEGEND

Jilted young women looking for love are heard to recite the phrase, "He loves me, he loves me not," as they carefully pull off one daisy petal at a time.

If they are lucky, they will have chosen a daisy with an odd number of petals and the flower will affirm the love of the man she longs for. But did you know that this practice actually was passed down from one gypsy generation to the next. Gypsies believed that a young woman could find her true love by sleeping with daisy root under her pillow.

FLOWER POWER

According to the month of your birth, these are your lucky flowers:

JANUARY: carnations and snowdrops

FEBRUARY: primroses

MARCH: daffodils

APRIL: daisies

MAY: lilies of the valley

JUNE: roses

JULY: water lilies

AUGUST: gladioli

SEPTEMBER: asters

OCTOBER: dahlias

NOVEMBER: chrysanthemums

DECEMBER: holly

HOW DOES YOUR GARDEN GROW?

You won't need a green thumb to work in these gardens.

Clear moon,
frost soon

- Never plant before the last frost in June.

- It is bad luck to plow the fields on Sunday.

- If it starts to rain while plowing, it's a sign of a good crop.

- Placing grain dipped in Holy Water around your house is said to protect it from burning down.

- Always plant cucumber seeds just before dawn.

- If you plant your beans before 9 am, you will be assured a healthy crop.

- Putting rusty nails in your garden will make the plants grow better.

- Crops that are planted on the 31st of any month will not grow.

- Plants will not grow if you thank the person who gave you the seeds.

Did you know...

that if you find a sand dollar on the beach, you should bring it home and put it in your garden for good luck?

Cathy Jones

Cathy Jones is a Gemini award-winning actor and writer and founding member of the award-winning comedy troupe CODCO. She is Canada's leading lady in character-driven comedy. Starring in the 17th season of the hit comedy series, This Hour Has 22 Minutes, Jones has revealed her remarkable ability to portray complex and difficult characters including the sassy suffragette Babe Bennett and the wise Mrs. Enid. Jones one-woman shows, "Wedding in Texas" and "Me, Dad and The Hundred Boyfriends" have sold out across the country. One of the longest running comedians on CBC Television, Jones has also starred in numerous short films, features and television series, including the lead role in the Mike Jones film, Secret Nation, which aired on CBC Television. Jones has received three Canadian Comedy Awards for best writing in a comedy series.

I grew up in a Catholic household in St John's, Newfoundland, and there were lots of sayings and beliefs about certain behaviors, which would make all the difference in how things turned out.

If you had your shirt on inside out in the morning, you left it that way because it was bad luck to change it.

If you pass someone on the stairs you both have to say "Bread and Butter." To this day, I can't pass someone without saying this and making them say it.

Crossed knives — there's gonna be a fight.

Bubbles on your pee — you're gonna come into some money.

If your palm is itchy — money is coming.

If you hit your mother your "hand would stick up out of the grave." (Nice!).

Then there were the warnings about your virtue:

"Why buy the cow when you can get the milk for free" and "No good locking the barn door after the horse is gone" And of course, "You can lock from a thief, but you can't lock from a liar."

And the usual warnings:

"Don't sit on the cold concrete, you'll get a cold right up thru ya."

"Handsome is as handsome does."

"Show me your friends and I'll tell you who you are."

"Mackerel sky never leaves the ground dry." A mackerel sky is that quilted looking generally speckled kind of sky. It's like a cloud covering with many fluffy uniformly distributed lumps.

IN THE LITTER BOX

Are the cats dumping in your garden? These suggestions may help.

- Spread mothballs around the ground.

- Pepper might also be a deterrent. Black pepper may work, but some say that chili or cayenne pepper works better.

- Place pieces of aluminum foil around your garden.

- Try sticking plastic forks throughout your garden, but they have to be close enough so the cat can't get between them.

- Plant garlic to deter cats.

- Sprinkle pine cones.

- Spread human hair around your garden.

- Try planting geraniums, marigolds and petunias. Cats don't like their smell.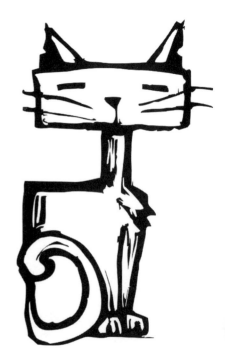

- Plant spiky plants throughout your garden, the cats will stay out.

- Spreading orange or lemon peelings throughout your garden is said to keep stray cats from turning it into a litter box. However, these will have to be replaced every couple of days as they dry out.

- Spreading coffee grounds over the ground will stop the cats from digging.

- Pipe tobacco may work. Chewing tobacco has also been suggested.

- Mouthwash, molasses, detergent and beer are all said to be good for keeping the cats away.

MAGIC MUSHROOMS

You may not want to use these mushrooms in your salad.

- Fairy rings, or large circles of mushrooms, were once believed to be the work of magic. Many thought misfortune. Perhaps serious illness or even death awaited anyone foolhardy enough to enter into the middle of such a natural phenomenon.

- It was once believed that serving mushrooms as part of your Christmas dinner would bring good fortune to your household.

- A house built in a field where fairy rings have grown is said to be filled with a happiness.

Chapter 7

Good Luck, Bad Luck

Believing in superstitions that bring us good or bad luck is something that is almost universal. These long-held beliefs cross over the generations and recognize no social, educational or economic boundaries.

Who hasn't heard that finding a four-leaf clover or carrying a rabbit's foot with you will bring you good luck, or that walking under a ladder will result in a plague of bad luck?

Most superstitions arise from incidences of repeated happenings and the emergence of patterns. For instance, if a hockey player doesn't shave prior to a game and his team wins, he draws a correlation between the two and he concludes that by his not shaving he has brought the team good luck. If he doesn't shave the next time he plays and his team wins again, then the pattern is reinforced. As long as man has been self-aware, he has looked for patterns in every day occurrences, patterns that might give him an edge in life and it is this that may explain the emergence of some superstitions.

One of the more widely recognized and revered good luck charms in the Atlantic region is the belief that horseshoes bring about good luck. In most barns throughout rural communities (and even in some homes), it is customary to affix a horseshoe over the door with the prongs pointing upward.

There are many theories as to the origin of the horseshoe superstition, but most involve the age-old battle against good and evil. One theory that dates back hundreds of years has it that a blacksmith in the "old country" encountered the devil at his door. The devil wanted to be "shoed." Upon recognizing the "evil one," the blacksmith tied him up and went to work, inflicting great pain on his visitor. The devil screamed for mercy, and the blacksmith released him, but only after the devil promised to never again enter a home protected by a horseshoe.

Another variation of this theory suggests that witches rode broomsticks because they were deathly afraid of horses. Therefore, a horseshoe is a good protective charm against witches. Horseshoes are made from iron, a good-luck metal, and they are crescent-shaped like the moon, which is a sign of prosperity.

And as to the question as to why a horseshoe is hung with the curve at the bottom?

Why to keep the good luck from spilling out, of course.

Just as there are universally recognized omens of good fortune, there are just as many signs of bad luck. The most common are: It is bad luck if a black cat crosses your path, when you knock over a salt shaker, open an umbrella inside, or break a mirror.

In Atlantic Canada, we tend to take it a step further. Not only do we recognize omens of bad luck but our beliefs are so ingrained that we embrace the notion that bad luck comes in a progression of threes. I heard that phrase uttered so often in my childhood that it has become part of my culture, just as it has for most people who have grown up in this region. I've discovered the existence of many theories as to how this belief came about. It may have something to do with the fact that three is the symbol of the Holy Trinity.

According to researchers, another tradition claims that the superstition of threes arose among British troops during the Crimean War. They learned from Russian captives of the danger of using any light for a threefold purpose and were told of the sacred rule of the Orthodox Church that only the high priest was permitted to light three candles on the altar from a single taper.

A more likely explanation of the origin of the custom is that British soldiers, entrenched against Dutch foes in the Boer War, learned by bitter experience of the danger of lighting three cigarettes from one match, thus giving a Boer sniper time to spot the light, take aim, and fire, killing the third man.

As with most superstitions then, we can see that even a simple saying such as "Bad luck comes in threes" evolved from more logical practices. As for the others, well, we're just not so sure.

A PENNY SAVED IS A PENNY EARNED

See a penny, pick it up, all day long you'll have good luck!
See a penny, let it lie, all day long you'll have to cry.

- If you have money in your pocket when you hear the first peepers in the spring, then you will have money all year.

- Money in your pocket on New Year's Eve, you'll have money throughout the coming year.

- If you throw a penny away, it will come back to you ten-fold.

- Burn the peeling from an onion and you will always have money.

- If someone gives you a coin on New Year's Eve, you should save it because it will keep giving you good luck.

- Never leave your pockets, purses or wallets completely empty, and never completely empty your bank account. Always leave at least a coin or two to replenish your funds.

- A gift of a wallet or a purse with a coin or two in it is good luck; bad luck if it is empty.

- It is bad luck to pick up a coin if it's tails side up. It is good luck comes if it's heads up.
- It is considered good luck to carry a penny in your shoe, especially if you have picked it up off the ground. That may be the origin of the penny loafer shoe.

- If you find a penny give it away to someone else for good luck.

DOWN UNDER GROUND

If you work as a miner, you may want to check out these pearls of wisdom.

- Miners believed that if they saw rats scampering to get out of the mine, they should also make for the exits as it was a sign that there would be a cave in.

- Miners believed that if a cat or dog crossed their paths while they were heading work, something bad would happen that day.

- Miners always lit candles in the mine. If the flame sputtered out due to insufficient oxygen in the air, they'd better get out.

- If a miner were to see a pig while on his way to work, he should miss his shift to avoid disaster.

- It was also bad luck to utter the word "pig" down in the mine, as it would cause a cave in.

- If a miner forgets something at home he should leave it there and go to work. It was bad luck for him to go back to get it.

Did you know...

that one should never stand in the middle when three people are being photographed, as the middle one will die first?

Wilfred Moore

Senator Wilfred Moore was appointed to the Senate by The Right Honourable Jean Chrétien as a representative of the Province of Nova Scotia on September 26, 1996. He is married to Jane Ritcey, of Lunenburg, who is also a long-time sailor in local and ocean waters, and they reside with their two sons in Chester.

- It is bad luck to launch a ship on a Friday.

- It is bad luck to have 13 characters in the name of a ship.

- It is good luck to have As in the name of a ship, especially three As.

The following are provided by my friend, Delbe Comeau, Meteghan River former First Mate in Bluenose II.

- It is bad luck to leave a hatch upside down because it could result in the ship being turned over.

- It is bad luck to have a total of 13 members in a ship's crew.

- When going aloft, it is bad luck to pass through the shrouds leading to the ratlines.

- One must always go around the shrouds, fore or aft, but never through them.

BY THE NUMBERS

You can count on these beliefs to hit the mark.

- One of the most widespread superstitious beliefs is that the number 13 is unlucky. For that reason, many hotels and office buildings do not have a room number 13 or a floor number 13.

- It is considered bad luck to have 13 guests at the dinner table. If need be, a 14th place should be set, even if it stays empty.

- It is believed that if 13 people are photographed together, one of those 13 will soon die.

- On the flip side, the number seven has long been considered a number of luck, wealth and power.

- People with seven letters in their names will be successful.

- Anyone born on the seventh day of the seventh month was considered to be posses special abilities, such as the gift of prophecy and communicating with spirits.

- Many people revere the number 12 because of the 12 apostles of Christ.

- The number 666 is feared by some because it said to the sign of the Devil.

Did you know...

that it was thought to be bad luck for a woman to enter a mine?

TAKE 5

Popular Maritime Good Luck Charms

In the Atlantic Region of Canada, many people believe these things will bring you good luck.

1. Wishbones
2. Horseshoes
3. Rabbit's foot
4. A falling star
5. A rainbow

TAKE 5 MORE

Popular Maritime Omens of Bad Luck

In the Atlantic Region of Canada, many people believe these things will bring you bad luck.

1. One crow
2. A black cat
3. Breaking a mirror
4. Birds hitting a house
5. Spilling salt

WHEN AT SEA

Fishermen are among the most superstitious people in the world. And with good reason.

- Whistling on the deck of a boat brings on a storm.

- Taking a woman on board a boat is considered bad luck.

- Many fishermen believe it is bad luck to bring bananas on board a vessel.

- It is considered bad luck to start a journey on a Friday.

- It is also thought to be bad luck to start a trip on the first Monday in April, the second Monday in August and on December 31st.

- Some fishermen believe it is bad luck to wear black on a boat.

- ome also believe it is bad luck to have people with red hair on board.

- You never step onto a boat with your left foot first.

- Throwing rocks in the ocean will bring on a storm.

- It is said that if the clothes of a dead sailor are worn by another sailor during the same voyage, tragedy will strike on board.

- When the rim of a glass rings it's a sign that there will be a shipwreck.

- It is a sign that a ship will be plagued with tragedy if the bottle does not smash during its launching.

- Mittens worn on a ship always had to be white. No grey was allowed because grey mittens brought grey skies.

- Dolphins swimming near a ship are believed to be good luck.

- It is bad luck to say the word "pig" on board a ship.

TAKE 5 . . .

- Pouring wine on the deck will bring good luck.

- It is unlucky to bring flowers on board a ship.

- It is considered bad luck to have a priest on board a ship.

- It is bad luck to look back once the ship has left port.

- Dogs on board a ship are bad luck but black cats on board are actually considered a sign of good luck.

. . . AND 5 MORE

- Seeing a swallow at sea is good luck but seeing a cormorant is bad luck.

- Losing a mop or bucket overboard is bad luck.

- Cutting your hair or fingernails at sea is bad luck.

- Hearing church bells while you're sea means someone on the ship will soon die.

- It is bad luck to say "drowned" while you're at sea.

ACCORDING TO LEGEND

Some early settlers told their children that witches lived in eggshells and that they made boats out of them. They would sail out onto the oceans in those boats casting spells upon the fishermen. The children were told that when they ate an egg, they should push their spoon through the bottom in the form of a cross before discarding the shell.

Philip Watson

Philip first went to sea at age 10 and has made sailing his life-long profession. He started working on board Bluenose II as a deckhand in the spring of 1987 and worked his way up to third mate, second mate and chief mate. He was made captain in 2001.

Sailors are a superstitious bunch and we take this stuff very seriously. Here are some of the most common ones that we follow very closely on board Bluenose II.

- Whistling is not permitted because it is said to bring on a storm. Only two people can whistle on a ship — the captain because he knows how to control the wind and the cook because it impossible to whistle while you're chewing - if the cook is whistling then he isn't eating. Any crewmember heard whistling will be asked to leave the ship.

- You never leave port on a Friday because it means you will have a bad trip and we try very hard to follow that rule. We would only set out on Friday on very rare occasions. Most times we would either depart no later than 11:59 p.m. on Thursday and no earlier than 12:01 a.m. on Saturday.

- It is bad luck to turn anything upside down on a ship because it simulates capsizing. You're not even to open a can upside down. It's so bad that I won't even do that when I'm on land.

- You never ring a bell unnecessarily on board a ship because it means a sailor somewhere it going to die. On Bluenose II we keep the bell wrapped in cloth and the clapper is kept secured. We only ring the bell when the occasion calls for it.

- You must never bring an umbrella on deck as it suggests that there will be a rainstorm and you don't want that when you're at sea. In fact, I'm so adamant about this one that I actually asked the King and Queen of Norway not to bring an umbrella on board during an official visit. They were all right with that because the King is a sailor and the Queen had just forgotten that umbrellas were bad luck.

- You must never wear black socks on board a ship because black is the colour of death and that could spell disaster for your voyage. It's okay to wear white, kaki, grey or navy, but never black.

- Always put a coin under the ship's mast to pay the ferryman when crossing the River Styx. When the mast is replaced on the Bluenose, so, too, is that special coin.

- You cannot say "pig" on board a ship. Now that's because pigs have cloves and hoof, supposedly reminding people of the devil.

- Whenever any alcoholic beverage is served on board a ship, before anyone else has a drink you must offer a drink to Neptune and to the ship's deck. It's a tradition honored on Bluenose II, on those rare and special occasions when alcohol is allowed.

- It is bad luck to stick a knife in the mast because it will bring on a big wind.

WHEN LADY LUCK SMILES

Good fortune could be just one good superstition away.

- Leaving the last mouthful of rum in the bottle will bring you good luck.

- It is a good omen if a tea bag breaks open in your cup.

- If a lace breaks while tying your shoe, it is considered good luck. To improve those chances of good luck, carry the broken lace around with you in your pocket.

- It is considered good luck to find two egg yolks within one shell.

- In some areas, it is good luck to carry an acorn with you.

- Good luck will come to your household if you own a three-coloured cat.

- Counting the cars on a train is said to give you good luck.

- It is good luck to wear a sock with a hole in it.

- It is good luck to spill wine while proposing a toast.

- Looking at the new moon over your right shoulder will bring you good luck.

- Finding nine peas in a pea pod is said to be a sign of good fortune.

- Picking up a pencil in the street is said to be good luck.

- Finding a five leaf clover is even luckier than a four leaf clover.

FIVER

One leaf for fame
And one leaf for wealth
And one for a faithful lover
And one to bring you glorious health
Are all in a four leaf clover

WHAT'S A FLUTTER YOU ASK?

These just might wing you some good fortune.

- If you find a floating feather it means you will soon come into money.

- It is considered a sign of good luck if a butterfly flutters around your head.

- It is considered good luck if a ladybug lands on you.

- If the first butterfly you see in the year is white, you will have good luck all year.

- Three butterflies together mean good luck.

See a pin pick it up,
And all day you'll have good luck.
See a pin let it lay,
And your luck will pass away.

ACCORDING TO LEGEND

Sing in the street, disappointment you'll meet
Sing before seven, you'll cry before eleven.
If you sing before you eat, you'll cry before your sleep.
Sing while eating or sing in bed,
Evil will get you and you'll be dead.

Chapter 8

Home Remedies

Shamans and medicine men, with their access to the world of good and evil spirits, have practiced healing for thousands of years. They would enter a trance state during a ritual and practice divination and healing. They used cures from the earth in the form of plants, animals, rocks, fire, smoke and even the sun and moon.

Dating back 5,000 years, records show that the Sumerians contributed some of the earliest known uses of medicinal herbs. There is documented evidence that the ancient Egyptians were using natural remedies as early as 1000 B.C. The use and cultivation of herbs for medicinal purposes is mentioned in the Bible's Old Testament. We also know that indigenous peoples relied on natural medicines, with some research confirming that these remedies were in use as early as 1900 B.C.

The Chinese are on record for documenting natural remedies as early as 2700 B.C. First Nations peoples of the Americas, Africa and Australia had also developed a strong tradition of utilizing herbal and natural remedies.

The ancient Greeks and Romans not only made use of medicinal plants but also traded with them. The World Health Organization estimates that to varying degrees, some 80 per cent of the world's population utilizes homemade remedies as their primary way of treating medical conditions.

FOOD FOR THOUGHT

The food you eat can do a lot more than make your stomach full.

- Eat fish to improve your brain power.

- Eating carrots will improve your eyesight.

- Eating onions will put hair on your chest.

- Cabbage is good for helping you lose weight.

- Eating garlic will help reduce your blood pressure.

- Eating liver will make you more fertile.

- Eating blueberries will help you maintain youthfulness.

- Oysters are an aphrodisiac. And so are peanuts.

- To cure diarrhea put nutmeg in your milk.

- To cure boils, soak a small piece of heel from the loaf of homemade white bread in boiling water. The older the bread, the better. Mix with a pinch of baking soda or salt. Squeeze the access water from the bread. Lay the warm mixture on sterile gauze or cloth securing it over the boil. Keep in place for several hours.

- Mixing a teaspoon of ground ginger in a glass of warm water and drinking it, will help cure stomach cramps.

- Drinking cranberry juice will cure bladder and urinary infections.

- An apple a day keeps the doctor away.

- Eating eggs will help prevent wrinkles.

- Lemons will help improve high blood pressure.

- When eating a fish, you should begin at the tail and work towards the head. This will bring you good health and good luck.

- Parsley or fresh mint will cure bad breath.

- Washing your hair in tea will clear up dandruff.

GOOD FOR WHAT AILS YOU

Don't try these at home.

- To cure an earache, blow smoke into it. Smoke from a pipe is said to work the best.

- Sealing hair clippings in bored holes in the front door will prevent asthma from inflicting the person whose hair was in the door.

- To reduce puffiness around your eyes, cover them with cool, wet tea bags.

- Rubbing cow manure on your head will cure baldness.

- To cure measles, boil sheep droppings and drink the "tea."

- Calm a toothache by placing a piece of tobacco or aspirin on the tooth.

- To stop the bleeding and pain from a cut, place an ax under your bed.

- Rub the blood from a cat's tail on the sores to cure the shingles.

- Wear a piece of lead tied to the end of a string around your neck to stop a nose bleed.

- Apply a spider's web to a cut to stop bleeding.

- Sitting on the cold cement or damp ground will give you hemorrhoids.

- Apply strong tea to a burn to prevent it from blistering.

- Use salt on mosquito bites to take away the itching.

- Also use salt to remove a leech to detach it from the skin.

- Bathe in milk to soothe the burning from a sunburn.

- Suffering from a planter's wart? Wrap duct tape around it and leave for several days.

- Diluted vinegar will cure an ear infection.

SAY GOODBYE TO THE STY

And give relief to your eye

- If you have a sty on your eye, place a piece of pork or raw hamburger over it and the sty will go away.

- Another way to remove the sty is to place a used tea bag over the infected area.

- Rub a wedding ring over the sty.

Did you know...

that washing your hands under moonlight cures warts?

Richard Crouse

Richard Crouse is the host of Richard Crouse's Movie Show on the E! Network and The Independent Film Channel. For ten years from 1998 to 2008 he was the host of "Reel to Real," Canada's longest running show about movies. He is the author of six books on pop culture history including "The 100 Best Movies You've Never Seen", "Reel Winners" and "Son of the best selling The 100 Best Movies You've Never Seen". He is the regular film critic for CTV's Canada AM and host of "Richard Crouse At the Movies" on CFRB NewsTalk 1010 in Toronto (also in syndication).

I don't consider myself a superstitious person but I grew up in Liverpool, Nova Scotia surrounded by people who said things like "Step on a crack, break your mother's back". Now, whether they really believed it or not, I don't know, but why risk something like that? If all it took to avoid a catastrophic injury was walking around the seams of the sidewalk who was I to disagree?

I don't really think that it's bad luck to say the word "pig" while fishing at sea any more than I believe that putting a mustard poultice on a wound will help it heal faster, but many years later I still think of these old wives' tales.

Birds seem to figure heavily in my memories of superstitions. I recall being told that if a bird flies into a room through a window, death will shortly follow.

I think my strongest memory of a Nova Scotian superstition wasn't a saying or omen but a silver ball that hung in the window of an old house near where I grew up. The Simeon Perkins House is a building preserved to depict life in Liverpool during the 1700s. In the window is a silver ball called a Witch Ball. The idea, as I recall, was that if a witch tried to enter the house she would see her reflection in the ball and get so freaked out that she would run away, leaving the residents to sleep safely in their beds. I'm not sure Witch Balls are very necessary in today's world, but I wish someone would invent some kind of Telemarketers Ball.

Terry Kelly

Terry Kelly's enthusiasm for life and sheer determination have gained him recognition as an accomplished athlete, an award-winning singer/songwriter, and entertainer. Terry was a double silver medallist at the 1979 Canadian Track Championships and a member of the Canadian Track Team that competed in the 1980 Paralympics. He has distinguished himself as the third blind person in the world to run the mile in under five minutes. Kelly has recorded six full-length albums, and has performed with Symphony Nova Scotia and the Edmonton Symphony. He has been nominated for four Canadian Country Music Awards and a JUNO. He is the recipient of seven East Coast Music Awards.

A number of years ago, I was traveling with my technician and guitar player from Halifax to St. Peter's, Cape Breton to do a show, when a bird flew directly into the path of my truck. The conversation we were having came to an abrupt stop. My guitar player became very quiet, and the air turned cold, and the truck was filled with an uncomfortable tension.

When I asked him what was wrong, he told me that the bird flying into our path was a sign that something was going to happen to someone close to him. When we arrived at our destination, I made a call to my office for something and was told that a very close musician-friend of ours had been in a serious car crash.

On a happier note - a friend and I went to visit an old fisherman buddy of ours to spend some time sitting on his boat yarning. He had a lovely bottle of Pusser's Old Navy Dark Rum sitting on the table, and he offered us a drop. After we accepted, he picked up the bottle, shook it vigorously, broke the seal, twisted off the top, then threw the stopper overboard. We asked him why he had done it. Smiling impishly, he told us that we were going to finish off the bottle that afternoon and wouldn't be needing the stopper. He also explained that he had to shake the devil out of the bottle before he opened it to be sure there would be no trouble.

Apparently, he knew what he was doing; there was no trouble!

As a very little boy growing up in St. John's, Newfoundland — in actual fact, I grew up between Halifax and St. John's — my Aunti Mimmie was able to encourage my cousins and me to stay out of the woods and away from the river by telling us that the fairies would take us away and we'd never be seen again. Although there did come a time when we figured Aunti Mimmie was pulling our legs, though took many years to be sure the fairies weren't lurking around the next turn on the path, or over there somewhere in the trees, especially at night.

A friend of mine in St. John's created and perpetuated his own superstition:-

One foggy summer night back in the seventies, a brother of a close friend of mine was driving along a road that skirted a lake. He missed a turn, the car flipped and trapped him in his car under water. He drowned. When my friend heard the news, it so happened the CCR song, "Bad Moon On The Rise," was playing on his car radio. From that time on and for a number of years, each time he heard the song he would become sad, reflective and sometimes angry. He believed that any negative happening was connected to the song.

I came to notice that if nothing untoward took place when the song came on, he would unknowingly create or initiate something with his girlfriend or maybe a scuffle in a bar with a stranger. I was three or four years younger than he was and somewhat impressionable. For a number of years I would also get an uneasy feeling and walk away or turn off the radio when I heard "Bad Moon On The Rise."

I don't walk away or turn it off any more.

A LITTLE STIFF?

These tips may loosen you up

- Carrying a potato in your pocket will help cure arthritis.

- Wearing a piece of cooper around your ankle will cure arthritis.

- Using ginger in your bath water will remove stiffness from your limbs.

- When you get a Charlie horse in your leg, quickly plant your feet on a cold surface and it will remove the cramps.

- Cooked beets will help treat arthritis.

BEATING THE COLD AND FLU SEASON

Something to sneeze at . . . perhaps.

- Feed a cold, starve a fever.

- For a high fever, tie an uncooked fish (preferably mackerel), to the bottom of both feet and cover them with a sheet. The fish will draw the fever from the body.

- Eating raw onions will prevent colds.

- Putting sulfur in your shoes will cure the flu.

- Drinking the juice from a cooked onion will cure a cough.

Did you know...

that rubbing mud on a bee, hornet or wasp sting will alleviate the stinging?

- Sleeping with a pair of scissors under your pillow will cure a headache.

- Rubbing a mixture of kerosene and butter on your throat and chest will cure a sore throat.

- Cut an onion in half and place the pieces under the bed to fight a fever.

- Drinking stock from home-made chicken broth will cure a cold.

- Horseradish will clear nasal congestion.

- Eating oranges will prevent the common cold.

BEET IT!

This red vegetable has its merits

- Eating beets will help cure constipation, treat arthritis and will lower high blood pressure and elevate low blood pressure.

- Drinking the juice from cooked beet greens will help cure the cold.

- To cure dandruff, mix some vinegar in a cup of beet juice. Massage the mixture into your scalp and leave it sit for about an hour, then rinse. Do this daily until the dandruff clears up.

Fact and Fiction

FICTION: Drinking black coffee will sober you up if you have been drinking.

FACT: It is widely believed that since alcohol is a depressant and coffee is a stimulant, the two will cancel each other out and you will sober up. In fact, you'll be wide awake, but you'll still be drunk.

THE POWER OF HONEY

Not only does honey taste good, but it is said to posses a powerful magic.

- It was said that sprinkling honey around a room on Sunday would drive out the evil forces and it would also kill all the pests that might nest there, a sticky solution.

- Feeding honey to cows was said to keep them healthy.

- Rubbing honey in the eyes of a sick cow would make it better.

- Eating a tablespoon of honey every day will ensure good health.

- Dumping honey down a well will keep the water pure.

- Blessing a field with honey will produce a healthy crop.

- Pouring a mixture of milk and honey in a hole in your garden will keep your garden healthy.

- It is bad luck to kill a honey bee.

Fact and Fiction

FICTION: Reading in low light will make you go blind.

FACT: There is no scientific or medical research to back up this claim. In fact, earlier generations did many chores by firelight and we've never heard of any of them ever going blind as a result. It is a fact that reading in low light can strain one's eyes, but you will not go blind.

WARTS AND ALL

These really get under our skin.

- To remove a wart, rub a piece of pork rind over it, wrap it in a piece of cloth and then bury the cloth. Over time, the wart will disappear. Another way to remove a wart is to rub a peeled apple over it and give the apple to a pig.

- Or half a potato is said to work just as well.

- Or rub the wart with a piece of bacon that was stolen from a neighbor.

- Or catch a frog and rub it on the wart.

- Or soak a wart in water in which potatoes have been boiled and it will go away.

- Or spread butter on the wart and have a cat lick it.

- Warts can be removed by touching them with a piece of string, tying a knot in the string for each wart and then burying the string in the ground.

- It was thought that warts could be cured by circling them in horsehair.

- It was believed that handling a toad will give you warts.

Did you know...

that placing a pot of honey in the centre of the Christmas dinner table is said to ward off evil spirits?

Chapter 9

Household tips

Eggs boiling dry in the pot. At some point in time, someone reached the conclusion that when that happens, it's a warning that a bad storm is brewing. It's possible that on the same day the pot went dry some sort of tragedy occurred and, as is often the case with superstitions, the correlation was made between the two. In time, as the story was retold and passed on from one person to the next, one event did seem to follow the other. A new "wives' tale" took root. The tip here, obviously, is to keep close watch on your pot while cooking eggs lest tragedy will surely enter your life.

Whenever she was cooking, my grandmother always maintained a vigil over her stove to ensure that none of her pots boiled dry, lest she bring bad luck down upon her household. Did that make her superstitious? Perhaps. But there's no question that it sure made her one of heck of a good cook.

Household beliefs and practices didn't end at the stove. In fact, even the most mundane and simple chores in many households in Atlantic Canada were carried out under a strict set of rules. Sweeping the floor, preparing meals and sewing are all subject to their own brand of magic.

For instance, if you don't want a visitor to come back, sweep out the room after he or she leaves and they'll never return. Legend also has it that it is bad luck to pass scissors from one person to another pointed-end first. It is also bad luck to leave your oven empty. Instead, use it as a place to store your pots. When you are sewing and your thread knots and tangles, someone is talking about you.

'EGGS'TRAORDINARY

Some people may get cracked up over these superstitions.

- Take a fresh egg into the fields in the spring to ensure a healthy crop.

- In the fall, crack a fresh egg in the garden to protect it from frost.

- Find two yolks in an egg and a pregnant woman will give birth to twins.

- Eating an egg a day improves a man's virility.

- A black spot on a yolk is an omen of bad luck.

- An egg with no yolk at all means a terrible tragedy is about to strike.

- Eggs laid by a white hen will cure stomach pains and headaches.

- An eggshell cracks while boiling, - expect a visitor to your home.

CLEAN SWEEP

Brooms are not just for cleaning. They are also powerful tools of prognostication.

- If you drop your broom in front of the door, you will have a visitor that day.

- Pick up a broom that has fallen over and you will have good luck.

- Sweep the dirt out the back door and not the front, or you will sweep away your friends.

- Sweep trash out the door after dark will bring a stranger to visit.

BAD LUCK BROOM

Beware of a sweep of bad luck.

It is bad luck to:

- sweep the floor on New Year's Day.

- carry a broom over your shoulder.

- pass a broom through an open window.

- step over a broom.

- borrow a broom.

- sweep before the sun comes up.

- sweep your floor after sunset as it will cause someone at sea to drown.

- lean a broom against a bed.

- take an old broom with you to your new house.

- empty your dustpan after dark, you'll throw away a friendship.

- sweep over anyone's feet, you'll sweep their life away.

Did you know...

that burying fish bones brings good luck?

CUTTING CORNERS

Don't run with scissors.

- Dropping a pair of scissors is said to warn that a lover is unfaithful.

- Breaking one blade of a pair of scissors is an omen of quarreling and discord; if both blades are broken at once; a calamity is to be feared.

- Scissors should always be sold, they should never be given.

- You will cut off your fortune if you use scissors on New Year's Day.

SEW WHAT?

PINS AND NEEDLES

See a pin and pick it up,
all the day you'll have good luck.
See a pin and let it lie,
luck will surely pass you by.

Fact and Fiction

FICTION: If you swallow gum it will take seven years to digest.

FACT: Gum will not break down and digest, but it will pass through the system in one lump, it will not take seven years.

- Never pass a needle from one person to another. Always stick it in a piece of fabric to pass it along that way.

- If you drop a needle, count to three for good luck before picking it up.

- Although it hurts, some say it is good luck to prick yourself while sewing.

- When darning a sock, always turn it inside out for good luck.

- It is bad luck to sew clothing while some one is wearing it unless the person in the clothes holds a thread in their mouth.

- Always sew a pillowcase on New Year's Eve to hold all of your troubles.

- Never leave sewing undone on New Years or it will stay that way for the next year.

- Never sew on Sunday because you will have to rip out all of those stitches when you get to heaven.

A STITCH IN TIME SAVED NINE . . .

Some things to keep in mind when you're on pins and needles.

- If you mend your apron or dress while you are wearing it, someone will lie about you.

- If you break your needle while making a dress you will live to wear it out.

Did you know...

that when cooking eggs, put a drop of vinegar in the water to prevent the shells from cracking?

- To upset a box of pins foretells a surprise as long as some of them are left in the box.

- If you tear a hole in a new dress the first time wearing it, you will have a new one before that one is worn out.

- Never start a garment on Friday unless you can finish it the same day.

- If you make a quilt or spread, be sure to finish it or marriage will never come to you.

Andrew Jackson

Andrew Jackson was born in Ontario but spent much of his childhood in the Kentville area of Nova Scotia were he completed his high school education. An actor on stage, screen and television, Jackson gained a steady fan base and wide exposure early on in his career with his role as Dr. Stephen Hamill on ABC's All My Children. He was subsequently cast in a large number of film and television productions. His film roles include Scooby Doo 2 and Edison (with Academy Award winners Kevin Spacey and Morgan Freeman), as well as appearing in Steven Spielberg's acclaimed sci-fi miniseries "Taken." His Canadian roles have included appearances in "Wind at My Back", "Being Erica" and "Sea Wolf."

I believe some people are more in tune with this sort of thing than others, but if you ask me if I believe in ghosts and superstitions, I would have to say yes. Maybe it had to do with where I grew up, but I remember people talking about signs of death and omens of impending tragedy.

And then when I went into acting, I became exposed to it all over again, because I've found that people, particularly those in theatre, who are really superstitious types. I've also found that a lot of the superstitions from theatre are much like those from the people

- When you are sewing and your thread knots and tangles, someone is talking about you.

- Never sew a button on a shirt while it is being worn or the person wearing it will have bad luck.

- Never begin to make a dress on Saturday or the wearer will die within the year.

who make their living on the sea. I think that's because historically, people who worked in the theatre also worked on the ships and the two just overlapped.

For example, it's bad luck to whistle on the set just as it's bad luck to whistle on the deck of a ship.

There was a time when it was bad luck to allow women on the set, just as it was bad luck on a ship to allow women onboard.

But the theatre does have its own superstitions as well, particularly when it comes to Shakespeare's play *Macbeth*. For example, it is considered bad luck to say "*Macbeth*" on set or in the theatre. If you do, you are supposed to leave wherever you are, turn around three times before returning. Apparently spinning around prevents terrible things from happening. If you are about to go on stage, you must never utter any lines or refer to the play (*Macbeth*) itself. If you must comment, then you must refer to it as the "Scottish play".

Also in the theatre, it is considered bad luck to put your shoes on the counter but it is considered really good luck if the costume maker bleeds on your costume.

And then, of course, there's that old familiar saying where telling an actor to break his leg before going on stage is actually wishing him good luck.

WHAT'S COOKING?

Something to sink your teeth into.

- Never ask, "What could go wrong?" in a kitchen because the recipe will ultimately fail.

- Never drop a knife in the kitchen.

- Drop a fork in a kitchen it means someone is coming to visit. Drop a spoon, then it's someone you haven't seen for some time.

- Never accept a utensil from another person once you have taken your place at the dinner table - expect bad luck if you do.

- To prevent them from burning, always leave the pot lid on when you're cooking vegetables that grow on top of the ground.

- To avoid shedding tears when peeling onions, always start at the root.

- Never hand someone else a knife in a kitchen. Lay it down and let them pick it up.

- Keep a cup of vinegar in the kitchen for good luck.

- Let a tea kettle boil and you chase away all your friends.

Did you know...

that in earlier generations, when a person was leaving a house and they had a bad feeling or a "haunting" as they called it, they would wipe their feet as they were leaving the house so the spirit would not follow them?

- Break up empty eggshells to bring good luck.

- Anticipate bad weather if you drop a glass of water in the kitchen.

TAKE 5

Good tips for the cook to heed.

- They say that if you chew gum while cutting up onions, you won't shed a tear.

- If gravy turns out lumpy, it means bad luck. In another version, lumpy gravy means a storm is brewing.

- Burning your potatoes is a sign that someone in the family is going to be ill.

- Never discard the wishbone from a turkey. Allow it to dry for good luck.

- It is bad luck to wear a hat in the kitchen.

- It is bad luck to sing at the kitchen table.

- Never leave an empty place setting at your table, lest you invite the Devil to eat with you.

YOUR DAILY BREAD

Who's making the dough?

- A cake baked in the afternoon will fall with the setting sun.

- A cake will fall in the middle if more than one person stirs it.

- Burn the bread and your family will go hungry some day.

- Brush crumbs from the table to the floor, you will always be poor.

- Never bake bread after sunset, it won't rise.

Chapter 10

Life and Death

A forerunner is a sign or warning of something to come. Atlantic Canadian legends are ripe with stories of those harbingers of impending disaster to our loved ones.

Being raised in a superstitious family these forerunners were taken seriously. My mother, like many of my female ancestors before her, was "tuned in" as they called it and paid serious heed to these warnings. Many times I heard my mother and grandmother talk about "seeing" people before they died even though there was no physical presence. Each of these stories would cause a shiver to race up my spine.

My mother told me of a 'happening' one Saturday afternoon some years ago when several members of the family were sitting around the kitchen table at the old family home enjoying a friendly game of cards. She looked up and noticed the figure of a man pass by the window. It was quick, but several others saw him as well. All heard the door handle jiggle and the latch lift three times as if someone were about to enter. No one came in. Everyone immediately agreed that they had just seen a forerunner. Although they had no idea who was about to die, they feared it would likely be someone within the family. The card game immediately folded-up and the group left quickly.

Lo and behold, three days later, one of my mother's favorite uncles suddenly dropped dead of a heart attack. Everyone who had been present for the card game that preceding Saturday concluded that it was the uncle's forerunner they had seen. The stuff of family legend, but this one scared the hell out of me.

FUN AT THE FUNERAL

There are certain rules for what you should and should not do at funerals.

- It is a commonly held belief that if you touch the deceased before the burial you will not grieve for them.

- If you kiss the deceased, it sends them into the afterlife without any regrets.

- Breaking into a funeral procession is bad luck.

- Seeing a crow at the grave site is a good sign.

- The eyes of the dead must always be closed or they will find someone to take with them.

- Women buried in black are said to return to haunt her family.

- It is not only disrespectful, but also bad luck to count the number of cars in a funeral procession.

- Bad luck will follow you if you do not stop the clock in the room where death has occurred.

- If death occurs in a house, all the windows and doors should be opened so that the spirit can get out.

- If you hold a funeral on a Friday, another will follow.

- You should never wear new shoes to funeral as it's a sign of disrespect for the dead.

- It is a good sign to hear thunder at a funeral.

- Pregnant women should not attend a funeral.

CEMETERY ETIQUETTE

Respecting the final resting place.

- It is best to avoid passing a cemetery on the way to church.

- Hold your breath when you pass a cemetery lest you breathe in the spirit of the deceased.

- Do not point at a cemetery or a grave.

- Never walk on a grave for fear of disturbing the dead.

- Tuck your thumbs into your fists when you pass a cemetery to protect your family from death.

MEETING YOUR MAKER

You may be closer to the other side than you care to know.

- Dreaming of the dead means someone close to you is going to die.

- Placing a hat on a bed is the ultimate in bad luck symbols. Someone you know will soon die.

- If a crow sits on your wash line in the morning, someone in the family will die that day.

- If you put someone's name in your shoe, that person will die

- When a sick person is on his or her death bed, animals should be kept out of the room. It was once believed that upon death, the spirit would enter the body of the animal.

THINGS THAT GO BUMP IN THE NIGHT . . .

May be trying to tell you something.

• If a window in your home suddenly slams shut on its own, someone is going to die.

• If a picture falls off your wall, it's a sign of death in your family.

• If a mirror that cracks or falls from the wall and breaks, means someone in the house will soon die.

• If a pot falls to the floor it means someone in the home will soon die.

FIVE MOST COMMON SIGNS OF IMPENDING DEATH

In the Atlantic Region of Canada, many people believe these things are a sign of an imminent death in the family.

1. A bird hitting a window
2. Seeing a forerunner
3. Window or door slamming shut
4. Putting a hat on the bed
5. A howling dog

Fact and Fiction

FICTION: When Shingles — caused by the reactivation of the chicken pox virus that leads to painful skin and nerve damage — meet at the waist, you will die.

FACT: The ailment is painful, but there are no recorded deaths in North America where shingles is listed as the cause of death.

MAN IN BLACK

From 1980 to 1982, I studied journalism in Lethbridge, Alberta and the incident in question occurred on a very cold evening in January 1981. I lived with several other college students in a large, rambling, three-storey, old home with a whole lot of character. It was Friday night and all the others had gone out for the evening, but I had decided to stay at home. Alone.

From where I sat in the living room watching television, I could see into the front yard from the large window that spanned the front of the house. A winding cement walkway led to a wrought-iron fence. At around 11 o'clock, as I happened to glance out the window, I watched as a tall, broad-shouldered man dressed in a long, black overcoat and a wide-brimmed hat opened the front gate. He came up the walkway and went around the side of the house to the back door. I thought that it was the landlord coming for a surprise inspection.

As I sat and watched the television, fully expecting the landlord to unlock the door and come in, it suddenly struck me that I hadn't heard any footsteps on the back stairs. Where could he have gone? If he had gone back out through the front gate, I would surely have seen him. The appearance of the mysterious man in black began to make me feel uncomfortable, and I experienced a strong sense of foreboding, as if something terrible was about to happen.

Hurrying to the back door, I peeked out through the frosted window glass expecting to see someone standing there waiting to be invited in. Much to my surprise, no one was there. Nervously opening the door, I stepped out into the cold night air and looked around the back of the house. Again, I saw no one. Quickly, I hurried back inside the house, but once inside I felt like my world was closing in on me. I knew there had been

Did you know...

that people in the Town of Lunenburg, like in most other early settlements, used to hold funerals from their homes. But did you know that they used to make one window in their homes larger than the others to allow coffins to pass through?

something unusual about the man, but I could not explain what it was or where he had gone. Not wanting to accept that maybe I had just seen something from beyond this world, I turned off the television and went to bed. I did not sleep well that night.

Two nights later I phoned my parents to see how things were back home in Liverpool. I asked my mother if everyone was all right. As I might have expected, she could sense something was bothering me and wondered why I would ask such a question. I then told her about my unexplained visitor.

"When did this happen?" she asked.

"Two nights earlier," I told her.

"What time?"

"About 11 o'clock," I answered.

Fred Hatfield

Fred Hatfield has been editor of The Vanguard newspaper in Yarmouth since 1979 but started working there in 1966 when the paper opened.

Superstitions? I'm sure there are more, but the one I recall well had to do with spinning a knife at a dinner table. Every time I would visit my grandmother as a kid and spin a knife on the table at dinner, she would snap at me to stop doing that because it meant a boat was sinking. Those were the only occasions when she would speak sharply or harshly to me. I haven't heard of that superstition anywhere else and I suspect (but don't know) that when a boat is encountering troubled waters, the captain has to be spinning the ships wheel around and around to stay steady. Maybe that's where she got that superstition.

I could tell by her sudden silence that something was wrong. She then told me that on the same evening I had seen the mysterious man at around two o'clock in the morning (11 o'clock in Alberta), my parents were awakened by my sister's screams from the next bedroom.

Rushing to investigate, they found my sister in tears and shaking like a leaf in a windstorm. When she calmed down, she told them that she had been sleeping but suddenly awakened with the feeling that someone had entered the room. At first, she thought it must have been either my mother or father or a friend who had been staying over in another room. When she opened her eyes, she was horrified to see a large man dressed in a long black overcoat and wide-brimmed hat standing at the foot of her bed looking down at her. She said the man disappeared when she screamed.

Putting the two stories together, my mother became convinced that something bad was about to happen. She felt the appearance of the man in black was a sign that someone in the family was going to die. The next day an uncle passed away.

Coincidence? Perhaps. Not for me.

Did you know...

that if a clock which has not been working suddenly chimes, there will be a death in the family?

Did you know...

that if a person who is buried lived a good life, then flowers will grow on his or her grave. If the person was evil however, weeds will grow?

Chapter 11

Natural Phenomena

My grandfather, god bless him, seemed to have a special bond with the earth, almost as if he had a personal pipeline to Mother Nature herself. I visited his farm often, and as a curious and impressionable youngster I devoured everything he said. He often talked about the "signs" that would guide us through our daily lives.

He told me many times that if one were tuned in to the world around him, one would see clues about what may lie ahead. Armed with that information, we could plan accordingly. It is unfortunate, but our attention to natural phenomena has dissipated with advent of technology. We no longer observe the skies or the subtle changes shown to us by Mother Nature, but rather depend on the weather channel or the observations of experts. We consume rather than participate.

Ancient cultures around the world were awake to the possibilities the natural world represented. Although many of those beliefs have been debunked or con-textualized by today's science, what has been lost today is the sense of awe and wonder and connection to nature that our ancestors were fortunate to have.

Storms and lightning, early arrival of animal life, and the volume of rain or snow were not events to be endured so much as accepted as the natural cycle of life. The universe was a place of give and take. For my grandfather and for me, it was a way of being part of world, not apart from it. It was a respect for and understanding of a world that is lost today.

In her groundbreaking 1980 book, *The Death of Nature*, environmental historian Carolyn Merchant reminded readers that up until the 1600s the Earth was alive, usually taking the form of a mother. She wrote that indigenous people the world over believed the planet to be a living organism, full of life-giving powers but also wrathful tempers. There were, for this reason, strong taboos against actions that would deform and desecrate her. Pay attention.

IF IT HAPPENS IN THE SKY

Look up . . . look way up and see what the stars are saying.

- If you wish upon the first star you see in the evening, it is said your wish will come true. The same holds true for wishing upon a falling star.

- Dogs (haze) around the sun means that it's going to rain.

- It is said to be bad luck when there is lightening in the sky but no thunder.

- A clear, star-filled sky on Christmas Eve is considered good luck by farmers. It is said to be a sign of a good crop in the coming summer.

- If pine trees are loaded with cones expect a long, cold winter.

- If holly bushes yield a low volume of berries, then expect a lot of snow.

RAINBOW AT NOON

Rainbow at noon, more rain soon.
Rainbow in the east, sailors at peace.
Rainbow in the west, sailors in distress.
Rainbow in the morning, farmers take warning.
Rainbow at night, farmers delight.

MOONSTRUCK

There's really more up there than just cheese.

- It is good luck to bow to the moon when you first see it in the evening.

- It was once thought unlucky to look at a new moon through glass.

- When there is fog and a small moon on the same night, a strong wind will follow.

- When the moon is low or at its brightest, the tides will be higher than normal.

- If the new moon is on Monday then the weather will be good.

- If a new moon occurs on a Saturday then there will be twenty days of wind and rain. If a new moon occurs on a Sunday, there will be a flood before the month is out.

- If a baby is born on a moonless night, he or she will not live to reach puberty.

- If there is no moon on Christmas Eve, the following harvest will be rich.

- A full moon brings on labor in pregnant women

TAKE FIVE

- The worst storms are likely to occur one to three days after a new moon and three to five days after a full moon.

- Sleeping in direct moonlight causes madness or blindness.

- They say the crazy people come out on the full moon of the month, hence the word lunatic.

- A wish made on a new moon will come true sometime within the next 12 months.

- Washing your hands under moonlight cures warts.

Carroll Baker

Carroll Baker began her recording career in Thunder Bay in 1970, and in 1972 she went to Nashville for her first session at the famed RCA "B" recording studio where all the greats had recorded, including Elvis Presley. That effort produced her first top-10 hit, and was the beginning of 12 consecutive number one records in Canada, a streak that has not been broken.

When I was growing up in Port Medway, I would say I was around 12 or 13 at the time, I had been out with a couple of my friends and came home with them after our walk. It was either late fall or early spring because the weather was cool, but not cold enough to have a fire in the kitchen all the time. My mom was visiting her mom, so it was just my friends and myself in the house, and although I had never lit a stove before, I was sure I knew how to do it.

We had a wood stove in the kitchen that had been converted into oil stove, so I took the lid off the stove, turned on the oil, lit a match and threw it in. My first attempt failed so I tried again without success it seemed, so I looked into the stove to see if I was doing something wrong.

At that moment the fire came up into my face. My cousin grabbed a towel wrapped it around my head and then took me upstairs to the bathroom so I could clean myself up. My eyelashes and hair were somewhat burned and my eyebrows were singed.

While I was standing looking in the mirror at the mess, something made me look toward the bathroom door, which I had left open. I saw the figure of a man standing in the doorway dressed in black with a black top hat on and a cane in his hand. I screamed so loudly that my friends ran upstairs and although they didn't see the man, I could see him as clearly as I could see them.

When my mother came home, I got into real trouble for literally playing with fire, totally deserved. I told her about the man I had seen. She told me I was not the only one who had seen the ghost-like figure in our home, that my sister Barbara had also seen him. There were stories that the house that had once stood on the property where our home was built was haunted and that the man I saw was the man who had lived in that house which had burned down many years ago.

RAIN OR SNOW

NATURE KNOWS BEST

But then, don't all mothers know best? When it comes to natural phenomena, this lady knows what she's talking about.

- The old saying goes, "Ash before oak, you're in for a soak." The idea here is that the ash and oak trees leaf-out at different times in the spring. Typically, the oak leaves appear full first, or in some years, at the same time as the ash. But if the ash leaves come out first, it means it's going to be a wet summer.

- In the Annapolis Valley, Nova Scotia it is said there are always three snowfalls after the equinox in March before it is truly spring. So predictable is this that the "Three Snows" have names — Smelt Snow, Robin Snow and Grass Snow. The first snow coincides with the smelt migration on rivers, the second with the first robins appearing in the spring, and the third is known as poor man's fertilizer.

- They say that if the first snow of the winter is subsequently washed away by rain, then the remainder of the winter will be open with little snowfall.

- For every instance of fog in August, there will be a snowfall in winter.

Did you know...

that placing an acorn in your window will prevent lightning from entering your house?

- If a squirrel buries a lot of nuts, it will be a hard winter. Or the higher up the nuts are stored, the deeper the snow.

- A bird call from the north means tragedy, from the south is good for crops, from the west is good luck and from the east good love.

- More molehills than usual? This is a sign of bad weather.

- Frogspawn at the edge of a pond. A storm is brewing.

- Ducks flapping their wings while swimming. A sign of rain.

EVENING RED

Evening red and morning grey
speed the traveler on his way.
Evening grey and morning red,
bring down rain upon his head.

Did you know...

that if you rake your yard before the first day of April, you will bring on the rain?

RAIN, RAIN GO AWAY . . .

Come again some other day.

No weather is ill,
If the wind is still.

- In summer, if leaves curl up so the underside is visible, it's a sign of rain.

- If all the cows in the pasture are lying down, it's going to rain.

- Hanging a Rosary beads on the clothesline on wash day would keep the rain from coming.

- If your pot of potatoes boils dry then it's a sign of major rainfall.

- When worms come to the surface of the ground in the daytime, it will rain.

- If horses are standing close together in the pasture, you should expect rain.

- Your cat sitting with its back toward a fire? It will rain.

- If a cat licks its tail, it's a sign of rain.

- Frogs croaking in daylight? Rain is coming.

Did you know...

that if the moon is red, there will be a strong wind?

POURING

It's raining,

It's pouring,

The old man is snoring.

He went to bed,

Bumped his head,

And couldn't get up in the morning.

Gerald Keddy

Gerald Keddy, Member of Parliament for South Shore - St. Margaret's, was born in New Ross, Nova Scotia, where he currently resides with his wife, Judy, and their six children.

During my lifetime, I have heard many superstitions and old wives' tales. Here are a few of my favorites:

Plant your potatoes or root crops in the dark or waning moon.

Peas, beans, corn . . . all those vegetables that grow in the sun, plant in the full or growing moon.

If you have a ghost, you can smoke it from your home with sweet grass.

A bird in the house is a forerunner of death.

If your butter turns sour, you have been cursed by a witch.

A ring around the moon means that a storm is approaching. The larger the ring, the further off the storm.

Never leave a cat near a sleeping baby as they "suck the breath" of the child.

SNOW DAY

What every kid dreams of.

- It is said that if children wear their pajamas backwards, there will be a major snowstorm over night and school will be cancelled the next day.

- Children can also try sleeping with their feet at the head of the bed and their head at the foot. It may also bring on a major snowstorm.

- Snowdrops are beautiful little white flowers that bloom in the late winter. They are said to be a symbol of purity and hope. However, if they are taken inside a house where there is a sick person it is an omen of death.

- Dreaming of snow is usually good luck.

- If there is thunder in February there will be a snowstorm in May.

- If there are two circles around a full moon, it is sign that it will snow within the next 24 hours.

- If snow sticks to the sides of trees, expect a long, cold winter.

- If there is snow at Christmas there will be a green Easter.

Year of snow,
Fruit will grow.

SUNSHINE ON MY SHOULDERS

When the sun comes out so too do the old beliefs.

- It was believed that babies born in the morning sunshine would live longer than those born later in the day.

- Babies born at sunrise will be more successful in life than those born at sunset.

- It is considered unlucky to point your finger at the sun.

- You should never stand in the direct sunlight at a funeral or you will be the next one to die.

- If the sun shines on a bride during the wedding ceremony, she will be blessed with a long, happy marriage.

- The sun will never shine upon a liar.

- If the sun shines through the apple trees on Christmas or Easter Day, the fruit will plentiful in the next harvest.

When the stars begin to huddle,
The earth will puddle.

Did you know...

that it is said that happiness and good fortune will follow if you see an albino robin or blue jay?

THE BIRDS AND THE BEES

These creatures are talking about more than sex.

- If a bird hits a closed window, it means someone close to you is going to die in the very near future. In a variation of this superstition in some circles, it is believed that the window must break before it's considered bad luck.

- If a bird visits your house on Christmas Day, that's good luck.

- If you see a bird flying during a snow storm, brace for a major snow fall.

- You know spring has arrived when you see your first robin. Make a wish and it will come true.

- If you hear a woodpecker you will soon coming into money.

- When hornets that build their nests close to the ground, there will be an open winter with little snow.

- An owl perched on your house is a sign of death.

- It is bad luck to see an owl in the daylight.

- The discovery of a dead bird on the ground is a harbinger of impending tragedy.

- If a bird flies into your house, someone close to you is going to die.

- It is bad luck to kill a sparrow as they are said to carry the souls of the dead.

- If a bee enters your house, it a sign that you will soon have a visitor. If you kill the bee, you will have bad luck or the visitor will be unpleasant.

- A swarm of bees settling on a roof is an omen that the house will burn down.

BIRDS OF A FEATHER FLOCK TOGETHER

Perhaps only they know why.

- If you see a flock of birds huddling together in the trees, head for cover because bad weather is about to strike.

- Three seagulls flying in a row is a sign of death.

- To hear three crow caws is bad luck.

- It is good luck for swallows to build their nests in your home. They protect it from fire.

WHEN LIGHTNING STRIKES

You'll want to take cover.
The sharper the blast,
The sooner it's past.

What not to do during a lightening storm:

- Open an umbrella when it is lightning.

- Sit on a toilet in the middle of a lightning storm.

- Stand under a tree in a lightning storm.

- Stand in a window during a lightning storm.

- Turn on a light switch during a lightning storm.

- Plug in or unplug an electrical appliance in the middle of a lightning storm.

- Stand in a water puddle in the middle of a lightning storm.

- Stand in high places in the middle of a lightning storm.

- Wear red clothing in a lightning storm.

- Use the telephone

Chapter 12

Not all Fun and Games

Sport is where some of the weirdest superstitions thrive as both players and fans have their ways of avoiding bad luck. Some sports superstitions are stranger than others, but all stem from a need to explain one's good or bad luck. Whether amateur or professional, athletes sometimes take it to the extreme.

Lawyers probably don't wear the same underwear everyday during a lengthy trial and when was the last time you saw a car salesman refuse to shave because he was on a winning streak, or a doctor follow the same routine every day because she felt it gave her good karma? In sports, however, this is situation-normal.

We've all seen athletes performing rituals before competition. We've heard stories about the baseball player with his lucky socks or the hockey player with his favorite stick or jersey or the golfer who will only wear a certain color of shirt on certain days. In pro sports, superstition and ritual are part of the appeal. To the observer, it may seem inane and strange, but if you consider how athletes use these rituals, you might see that many of them are strategies or processes developed to help them win or focus.

Superstition in sport arises when an athlete has a particularly good (or bad) performance and then tries to establish "cause and effect" by reviewing the facts of the day. They take note of what they ate or wore, and pay particular attention to anything unusual that happened such as getting a haircut, receiving a gift or hearing a certain song. If they have a great performance, they attribute their success to that unusual circumstance and attempt to recreate it before every competition.

Sport in Atlantic Canada also takes place on the kitchen table. And perhaps nothing carries more clout in these parts than those superstitions that govern our card games. My grandmother, for example, was so adamantly opposed to anyone playing cards in her house on Sunday that she forbade anyone to even suggest it. It is interesting how those images from our childhood remain so strongly etched in our minds.

GONE FISHIN'

The dos and don'ts for catching — and losing — the best fish

When the dew is on the grass,
rain will never come to pass.

- Throw back the first fish you catch and you'll be lucky the whole day.

- Fish bite best at night during full moon or after a hard rain.

- If you dream of fish, someone you know is pregnant.

- It is bad luck to get married when the fish aren't biting.

- If you fish for the first time in the season on Good Friday, good luck will follow you throughout the season.

- It is unlucky to fish with your lines crossed.

- If the end of your pole touches the water, you should just go home as you will catch no more fish that day.

- Never fish on Sunday because it will bring bad luck.

- Fish may not bite if a barefoot woman passes you on the way to the dock.

- If the cows are standing in the pasture, it's a good day to go fishing.

Did you know...

that it is bad luck if someone steps over your fishing line?

A WHOLE LOT OF SHAKIN' GOIN' ON

Getting hooked on good luck.

- If you dig your worms before sunrise, you will catch more fish.

- Spit on your worm after you have put it on the hook for good luck.

- It is bad luck to dig your worms from your flower garden, but good luck to dig them from your vegetable garden.

- It is unlucky to bait your hook with a worm by using your left hand.

YOU KNOW YOU'RE IN TROUBLE WHEN . . .

The big one got away . . .

- It is considered bad luck to wear black when you go fishing.

- If you fish against the wind you will have better luck.

- You should never let your shadow fall on the water while you are fishing or you will scare away the fish.

- If you count the number of fish you have caught, you will catch no more for the remainder of that day.

- Sit on an upturned bucket while you are out fishing.

- It is bad luck to take a dog on a fishing trip.

- If you swear while you are fishing, you will go home empty handed.

- It is bad luck to change poles while fishing.

BE A GOOD SPORT

There are the official rules of the game and then there are "these" rules.

In baseball

- Spitting into your hand before picking up the bat is good luck.

- It is good luck to stick a wad of gum on your hat.

- A dog walking across the diamond before the first pitch is bad luck.

- Some players believe it is good luck to step on one of the bases before running off the field at the end of an inning.

- It is bad luck to touch the baselines while running off and on to the field between innings.

- Your game will be jinxed if you lend a bat to a fellow player, but good luck to lend your glove to another player.

- If a pitcher is throwing a perfect game or a no-hitter, never speak to him or you'll break his luck.

Did you know...

that most people associate the Ace of Spades as the ultimate bad luck card as it foretells death and tragedy, but in truth the Four of Clubs is just as ominous. Once known at the Devil's Bedpost, it was considered particularly unlucky to draw that card during the first hand of any game?

In basketball

- The last person to shoot a basket during the warm-up will have a good game.

- Wipe the soles of your sneakers for good luck.

- Bounce the ball before taking a foul shot for good luck.

- It is bad luck to tie your sneakers on the basketball court.

- It is bad luck to pass a basketball to another player once you enter the court. Toss it or bounce it instead.

In bowling

- To continue a winning streak, wear the same clothes at every game.

- Carry charms in your bowling bag, in your pockets or around your neck for good luck.

- It is bad luck to pass a bowling ball to another person.

- It is good luck to wipe the soles of you bowling shoes before stepping onto the lanes.

- It is bad luck to chew gum while bowling.

Golf

- Start only with odd-numbered clubs.

- Balls with a number higher than four are bad luck.

- Carry coins in your pockets for good luck.

- It is bad luck to toss your clubs on the ground.

- It is good luck to wear red if you golf on Sunday.

Hockey

- It is bad luck for hockey sticks to lie crossed.

- To say "shutout" in the locker room before a game is bad luck.

- Players believe they'll win the game if they tap the goalie on his shin pads before a game.

- Many players believe putting their pads and skates on in exactly the same order every day will give them good luck.

- It is bad luck for the goalie to put on his mask before going onto the ice.

Tennis

- It is bad luck to hold more than two balls at a time when serving.

- Avoid wearing the color yellow on the court because it will give you bad luck.

- Walk around the outside of the court when switching sides for good luck.

Did you know...

that while playing cards it is bad luck to whistle?

- It is bad luck to step on the court lines.

- Lending your tennis racquet to another player is bad luck.

IN THE HUNT

Planning on heading into the woods? Be careful.

- You should always carry a rabbit foot for good luck when you are hunting.

- If you see your shadow while you're hunting, it is bad luck and you will go home empty-handed.

- Firing three times and missing means your hunting season is over.

- If you kill the first rabbit you see on your first hunting trip of the season, you will have good luck throughout the season.

- Never load your gun until you reach your hunting destination or you will have bad luck.

- Once you've started out on your hunting trip, never go back home for something you may have forgotten, or you will have bad luck and will return empty handed.

- You will have bad luck if you step in the paw or hoof prints of the game your are hunting.

- If you wrap a black horsehair around your wrist you will shoot straighter.

- It is good luck to carry raisins into the woods when you go hunting.

- It also good luck to carry apples with you.

- It is bad luck to go hunting on Sunday.

Glen Murray

Glen Murray was raised in Nova Scotia area and played junior hockey for the Sudbury Wolves of the Ontario Hockey League (OHL). He was a first-round draft pick, 18th overall by the Bruins in the 1991 NHL Entry Draft. He spent four seasons with the Bruins before being traded to the Pittsburgh Penguins. Murray's stay with the Penguins only lasted a little over a year and he was eventually on the move again. This time he was traded to the Los Angeles Kings. He enjoyed moderate success with the Kings, picking up some good numbers during his five-year stay, but on October 24, 2001, he was traded back to the Boston Bruins. Murray enjoyed his greatest offensive season in 2002–03, scoring 92 points (44 goals and 48 assists) for the Bruins and earning a spot in the 2003 NHL All-Star Game. On July 23, 2008, the Bruins placed Murray on waivers, and three days later, on July 26, the Bruins announced the buyout of Murray's contract to free up salary cap room. In November 2008, Murray had ankle surgery and has not played in the NHL since.

Here are some of the things we hockey players like to call "routines" but they're really superstitions.

First off, if you win you must continue to do everything exactly the same or else you break the streak of good luck.

EXAMPLES: What time you left for the game. What suit and tie you wore, socks, shirt, underwear and shoes. When I say everything that means everything. So if you see a hockey team on a winning streak and if it's a long one - you can just imagine.

What I noticed over the years that I played is that the coaches are just as superstitious as the players are, if not more.

EXAMPLES: Team meetings are always held at the same time. If we're on a winning streak, however, the coaches made sure that all meetings ended at exactly the same time as the first meeting, right down to the minute. Each person had to sit in the same place for every meeting.

As for myself, if I had a good game and felt good that night, I would keep that routine or superstition going until I felt the luck had run out. For my whole career I always stepped into the arena and onto the ice for practice and games with my left foot first — always.

Now when it came to putting my equipment on that was a whole different beast. There are game clocks in every NHL locker room. They count down to when we are to be ready to go on the ice for the start of the game. I always dressed, as you might have guessed, starting with the left side first. I would not start tying my skates until a certain time every game. I played with guys who would not start tying until we actually started walking out for the game.

Now when we warmed up for the game there was a lot of superstitions including who would shoot first, who would pass the pucks, what time we finished, and who would come off the ice first. It could even extend as far as to what fan you might want to give the puck to in the stands.

For the most part, a lot of the teams would stick with the same routines for every game. If the team would go on a bad losing streak that's when things would be altered in an effort to find that winning edge again.

IT'S IN THE CARDS

Who's really playing that game with you?

- If you play cards on Sunday, you play with the Devil and bad luck will follow you for the next week.

- It is bad luck for you to drop a deck of cards.

- Never take a deck of cards from anyone another person's hands or they'll pass the devil over to you.

- At one time, it was thought to be bad luck to have a dog in the same room where cards were being played.

- It was once thought to be bad luck to play a game of cards on a bare table. The table should always be covered.

- Some people believe that drawing a pair of red Jacks suggests that someone you are playing with is actually an enemy, even if they seem like a friend.

- It is bad luck to deal out the cards in an anti-clockwork direction.

- It is bad luck to ask another player what cards they are holding.?????I guess

Unspoken rules for playing cards

> Never look at your cards until the dealer is finished.
> Never pick up your cards with your left hand.
> Never whistle while you're playing cards.
> Never walk around the card table during the game.
> And finally, never, ever swear while you are playing cards or you invoke the Devil.

THE WHOLE WORLD'S A STAGE

Having good luck in theatre is not as simple as breaking a leg.

• When applying your makeup it is good luck to get lipstick on your teeth.

• Always leave the dressing room with your left foot first, but have visitors enter with their right foot first.

• It is good luck to be pinched.

• Having a cat in the dressing room is good luck.

• Finding a piece of lint on another actor's costume is good luck.

• It is bad luck to put shoes on a chair or counter in the dressing room.

• It is bad luck to have real flowers on the stage.

• Never open a play on the 13th day of any month.

• Never allow another actor to look over your shoulder into the mirror while applying your makeup.

• Green is not a particularly lucky colour to wear on stage.

Did you know...

that it is good luck to see three ducks fly over while you are hunting but it is bad luck to shoot those ducks?

Chapter 14

Omens

Did you know that dropping a dishcloth to the floor actually means a stranger is going to visit your house? It's true. My dear mother would literally fly into a tizzy if ever she dropped the dishcloth, as she thought it was a sign that someone would soon visit. She fretted that maybe the house wasn't tidy enough for company. In her world, and the world of many other Atlantic Canadians, dropping a dishcloth is an omen.

By their very name, most omens have an ominous nature and for good reason. Most omens in Atlantic Canadian folklore have to do with death and destruction. Most are precursors to tragedy and those who pay attention to such things are usually left shaken.

But not all omens are bad.

Omens are essentially events or occurrences that are thought to foretell the future. They often signal the beginning of a great change, and though many people feel cautious about bad omens and what they might mean, the fact is that some omens could traditionally foretell good things as well.

Dreams are a good case in point. Some people believe that our dreams are actually omens. Most cultures are known to use omens, and in some cases the omens were used to predict the actions that a great leader might have taken. Some of the earliest mentions of omens in human history come from the ancient Romans. Omens were such an important part of the Roman public and private life that there were two types of omen readers. Haruspices found omens in the entrails of sacrificial animals, while augers found them in the flight of birds.

According to historical records, these offices were held in high regard and would be consulted before any major event. During times of peace, they might foretell the perfect day for weddings or festival, and during more turbulent times they might decide when the city went to war.

But the Romans were not the only people who believed in omens and what they might mean. The ancient cultures of India, China, South America and First Nations peoples all have stories of their own that speak to omens.

Astrological phenomena were often associated with events that were going to happen. Halley's Comet was recorded on the Bayeux tapestry, for example, and there are many people who saw it as a hint of great things to come.

Omens have played a significant role in the history of the world. They taught us to pay attention to the future.

IN YOUR WILDEST DREAMS

What are your dreams really telling you?

• If you dream you are falling, it is a sign of death.

• If acorns appear in your dreams, that is a sign of good luck.

• Dreaming of angels is a sign of success and happiness.

• Dreaming of the dead means someone close to you is going to die or you will hear from a long-lost friend or family member whom you haven't seen in many years.

Did you know...

that dreaming of horses means that someone is on their way to visit?

- A cat in your dream signals that something evil has entered your life. If you dream about a white cat, good luck will follow.

- Dreams of birds, particularly crows or owls, means you will soon receive some bad news. But if those birds are doves or sparrows, that is good news.

- If you dream of running water, it means you are going to take a trip on a boat.

- Dreaming of flowers is a sign that you will soon attend a funeral.

- If you dream of a baby then death is near, but if you dream of death, it means there will soon be a new baby in your family.

Did you know...

that you should never turn your mattress on a Sunday or change a bed on Friday or you'll have bad dreams?

TEN MOST COMMON LIVING
THINGS IN MARITIME SUPERSTITIONS

In the Atlantic Region of Canada, these living things often foretell of doom and gloom, and sometimes, good luck.

Crows

Cats

Bees

Dogs

Cattle

Hens

Spiders

Horses

Crickets

Gulls

Did you know...

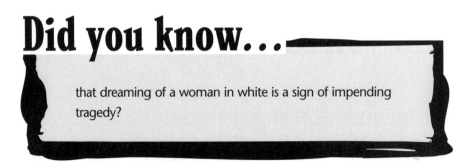

that dreaming of a woman in white is a sign of impending tragedy?

Nancy Regan

Nancy Regan is a broadcast and communications professional with 15 years experience on live television. Her on air warmth and humour have been her trademarks. As the longest serving host of CTV's Live at 5, she was an integral part of one of the most successful and highly rated news programs in Canada. Regan has also served as the host of Good Morning Canada, CTV's national weekend morning show. In addition to being a very busy mother of two boys, Regan now does freelance television work, professional speaking, media consulting and acting. Her passion for acting has led to professional roles on stage and in television movies and series.

I sometimes wonder if my children will carry my superstitions with them into adulthood. I wonder, for instance, whether having been told to lift up their feet every time they drove over railway tracks, would stay with them. Whenever I have a new friend in the car for this ritual, they invariably ask why. We explain that while some people consider it bad luck not to lift them over the tracks, we prefer to think of it more in terms of good luck if you do!

Everyone in our home knows that shoes are never to be put on a bed, table or even a counter as it clearly is asking for trouble.

And if I walk out the door of the house to be confronted by one crow, I almost always take the time to find another . . . harking back to the saying, "One crow, sorrow; Two for mirth, Three for a wedding, Four for a birth, Five for silver, Six for gold, Seven for a secret not to be told."

If anyone sneezes in a room I'm in, I feel compelled to say "God Bless You," and while I'd like to say that's born of deep faith, it may be more accurately described as superstition mixed with compassion.

And hmmm, number five. I'm not sure I have a number five. Oh wait! I do. Often, when I get change from a cash purchase which includes a penny, I will discreetly drop a copper on the ground so that someone will be able to "pick it up, and all day have good luck."

When I started this process, I was sure I couldn't fulfill the assignment of completing a list of five superstitions, but now I'm concerned that I will continue to realize just how many others are part of my life.

WHERE'S THERE'S SMOKE

If you play in this fire, you might just get burned.

- If a fire hisses while it is burning, misfortune is about to strike someone in the household.

- Sparks generated by a fire? The person in whose direction those sparks fly will soon receive some good news.

- It is bad luck to throw money in a fire.

- If the smoke from a fire rises straight up, the weather will remain calm for the next 24 hours. Conversely, if the smoke lays low and spreads out, you should expect a storm within the coming 24 hours.

YOU'VE GOT COMPANY

Are you expecting visitors?

- Setting an extra place at the dinner table will invite the friendly spirits to stay for a meal.

- If you drop a spoon, a child will visit your house.

- If you drop a fork, that visitor will be a woman.

- Dropping a knife. You can expect that visitor to be a man.

Knife falls, gentleman calls,
Fork falls, lady calls.
Spoon falls, baby squalls.

Chapter 15

Special Occasions

Consider this: Open the back door of your house before midnight on New Year's Eve to chase out all the stresses, worries and unhappiness of the old year, then on the stroke of midnight open the front door to allow good fortune and joy to enter and take up residence there.

Or this: It is considered good luck if the first visitor to your house on New Year's Day is a tall dark and handsome man bearing a gift, whether it be a piece of coal or a stick for the fire.

And from our childhood, we all know that if you blow out all the candles on your birthday cake with one breath while making a wish, that wish will come true.

Special occasions and holidays are an important part of our lives. Festive days are often shared with friends and family and celebrated with special foods and decorations. In many of these celebrations, there are traditions that are strongly connected with religious belief, but we also find that within this rubric there is a strong thread of mysticism.

The roots of many of our modern holiday traditions can be traced back to their pagan roots. In the Northern Hemisphere, the celebration of the winter solstice, known as Yule, is one of the oldest celebrations in the world, and is held to commemorate the shortest day and the longest night of the year. The tradition of hanging mistletoe can be traced back to these ancient celebrations when Celtic priests or Druids would cut the sprigs of mistletoe they found growing on oak trees and give it as a blessing to their people. In pagan belief, oaks were seen as sacred and mistletoe, the tree's winter fruit, was viewed as a symbol of life.

The tradition of kissing under the mistletoe evolved from the Celtic and the Nordic people who believed that mistletoe had magical, medicinal and aphrodisiac properties. The feuding Norsemen also considered mistletoe as a symbol of peace.

If by chance they happened to encounter mistletoe growing nearby, they kissed and made up, or they put away their weapons to fight another day.

Here in Atlantic Canada, we not only continue to observe these age-old traditions, but we've also created many of our own.

'TIS THE SEASON

Santa Clause may come on Christmas Eve, but your choice in which superstitions to follow will determine if your holiday will be good or bad.

- Lucky are those who are born on Christmas Eve or Christmas Day.

- Don't wash a Christmas present of clothing before gifting as that washes away the good luck.

- The gender of the first visitor to your home on Christmas Eve predicts the sex of the child of any pregnant women in the household.

- Weather conditions at the Christmas season can tell us a great deal – a blowing wind on Christmas Day brings good luck. Snow on the ground on Christmas Eve is lucky

- In some households, it is a tradition that the oldest person in the home should open their Christmas gifts first followed by the youngest. After that, the order does not matter.

- Place acorns on your Christmas tree for luck.

- Hang a wreath on your door at Christmas to welcome to all those who enter.

- Place holly around your house at Christmas to bring good luck. It will also keep the witches away during the Christmas season.

HAVE A HOLLY, JOLLY CHRISTMAS . . .

These things you can do without. They are all bad luck!!

- Singing Christmas carols at any other time of the year.

- A dog howling on Christmas Eve.

- Consuming alcohol on Christmas Eve.

- Going fishing on Christmas Day.

- Having your Christmas tree fall over, someone you know will soon die.

- Washing clothes on Christmas Day will cause a boat somewhere to sink.

NOT SO BAH ... HUMBUG

Some things to consider in planning that festive dinner

- The Christmas dinner table was always set for an even number of guests as odd numbers were said to bring bad luck, even if it meant leaving one place unused. The traditional dinner consisted of 12 courses for the 12 Disciples.

- Placing a bowl of garlic under your table for your Christmas dinner will bring you strength and protect your family throughout the coming year.

- Place fish scales under your Christmas dinner plates for good luck.

- Place a pot of honey in the centre of the Christmas dinner table to ward off evil spirits.

- To protect your house from burglars or intruders, tie a piece of string to a leg of the table where you eat your Christmas dinner.

- Diners must wait at the table until everyone completes their Christmas dinner or bad luck will befall the household.

- A loaf of bread left on the table after Christmas Eve dinner, will ensure a steady supply of bread for the next year.

John Leefe

John Leefe is an author, former teacher and politician. Leefe represented Queens County in the Nova Legislature from 1978 to 1999. He is currently the Mayor of the Region of Queens.

We remember stories and sayings told by our grandparents and their friends – some are from Saint John where I grew up, some are from Summerside where my wife Nancy was raised.

If you don't eat bread with corn on the cob you will throw a fit.

If you don't wait an hour to go swimming after a meal, you will get cramps and drown.

Always cover your head in cold weather to keep your body from losing heat.

Don't let children eat candy because the sugar will make them hyperactive.

To cure arthritis you should wear a copper bracelet.

To get rid of a wart, spit on it first thing every morning.

If you hear three knocks and there is no one there, someone close to you is going to die.

THE MYSTICISM OF FIRE

and reading its signs during the holiday season.

- It is considered good luck to keep a fire burning in your house during the 12 days of Christmas.

- Having difficulty lighting a fire on Christmas Day is a sign that you will have bad luck for the remainder of the year.

- Burning old mistletoe was said to predict marriage prospects of an unmarried girl. Steady flames were said to ensure a happy married life while the sputtering flames predicted a rocky union.

- In modern times, we use Canada Post to get our letters to Santa, but in earlier times it was a tradition to burn the Christmas letters on the fire so that they would be magically transported by the wind to the North Pole.

- Placing lit candles in your windows on Christmas Eve will help guide lost loved ones back to your home.

- Keeping a candle lit throughout Christmas Eve will bring good luck to your household. But, if that candle goes out during the night, it's a sign of bad luck.

Did you know...

that at one time, unmarried girls would steal sprigs of mistletoe from church decorations at Christmas time and hide them under their pillows because they believed it would cause them to dream of their future husbands?

Peter Zwicker

Peter Zwicker was born, raised and educated in Lunenburg. He returned to Lunenburg in 2004 and is active in community affairs serving on town council and as a volunteer with a number of community organizations.

When going to school at the Lunenburg Academy, a dark and daunting building even then, my friends and I believed there were ghostly figures inhabiting the dark, dank and scary basement. To add to our fear and trepidation, we had to pass the Gallows Hill on the way to school, where we were told that people had been hanged for a variety of crimes.

If you could skip a rock through the crest of a wave you would be able to cut the devil's throat.

A loaf of bread always had to be right side up in the breadbox. If the loaf were upside down it would be bad luck for vessels leaving port and symbolized a capsized vessel. Amazing how this sticks with you over the years.

Perhaps this was more of a saying than a superstition or old wives' tale, but I remember as a child saying this rhyme, "Don't say ain't, your mother will faint and your father will fall in a bucket of paint."

Walking home from school as elementary students we had to avoid stepping on cracks in the sidewalk. If we stepped on a crack, we were warned that it would break our mother's back.

I recall that in Lunenburg it was bad luck to leave a home through any door other than the one you entered. To this day I generally enter and leave a home through the same door.

Similar to the door story above, another old wives' tale applies to beds. You need to get out of the same side that you get in or you will have bad luck.

When a cup of coffee is poured and it foams or bubbles on the top, it is a sign that you will come into money. Grab a spoon and scoop as much of the foam out of the cup to preserve the money for you.

If you swallowed gum it was believed that it would clog up your system and wouldn't pass.

I still knock three times on wood if speaking of something that might bring good fortune or to prevent bad luck.

Taking a cat on-board a vessel was always deemed to bring good luck. A friend reminded me of a few others that she recalled from her mom, who would not pass someone on the stairs, put up an umbrella in the house, walk under a ladder and always had to find the second crow.

SPOOKY STUFF

What you should really know before you go trick-or-treating.

- While black cats are considered bad luck on most days, it is actually good luck for a black cat to cross your path on Halloween.

- If you gaze into the flame of a lit candle on Halloween you will see into the future.

- If the flame on a candle suddenly goes out by itself on Halloween, it is said that a ghost has come to visit.

- For good luck, light a candle on Halloween, but do not burn that candle at any other time of the year.

- A person born on Halloween is said to be able to see and speak with spirits.

- A bat flying around your house on Halloween, means someone you know will soon die.

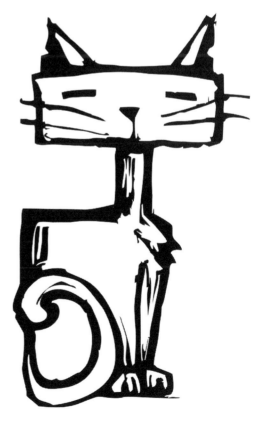

- Bury animal bones or place a picture of an animal near the doorway, to prevent ghosts coming into the house on Halloween

- Bats flying vertically upwards then dropping back to earth means 'The Witches Hour Has Come'.

Good To Eat
Trick or treat,
Smell my feet.
Give me something good to eat.

THE MOST HOLY OF DAYS

Good Friday and Easter days in the Christian faith, but what other meaning do they carry?

- A child born on Good Friday and baptized on Easter Sunday is said to have the gift of healing.

- Many fishermen will not set out to sea on Good Friday because tragedy will befall the voyage.

- Crops should never be planted on Good Friday as there is an old belief that says no iron (shovel, spade, etc.) should enter the ground on this most holy of days.

Did you know...

that bread or cakes baked on Good Friday will not go moldy?

- Hot cross buns baked on Good Friday were said to have magical powers.

- Eggs laid on Good Friday will never go bad.
- Hardened, old hot cross buns are supposed to protect the house from fire.

- Sailors took hot cross buns to sea with them to prevent shipwrecks.

- A bun baked on Good Friday and left to get hard could be grated up and put in some warm milk to ease an upset stomach.

- Having a hair cut on Good Friday will prevent toothaches the rest of the year.

- For good luck during the year, wear new clothes on Easter Sunday.

- The spirit of a person who dies on Good Friday will go directly to heaven.

- Never do laundry on Good Friday or you'll wash a member of your family away.

Chapter 16

What Evil Lurks

Of all the superstitions that have been handed down through the ages, none carries as much clout or reverence as those that warn us that evil is in our midst. These beliefs have existed for centuries, some dating back to the dawn of time.

Babylonian and Assyrian priests, for example, predicted tragic events by relying on signs seen the behavior of animals, birds, fish and reptiles. The revered elders also studied the entrails of sacrificial victims for clues as to what evil may lurk amidst their people. The appearance and condition of human and animal offspring at birth also provided them with warnings that something evil was or was not afoot.

Earlier civilizations recognized signs by studying the symptoms of sick people, the events or actions in a person's life, dreams, visions or something as simple as the appearance of a man's shadow. They also took their cues from fire, flame, light, smoke and from nature - fields, marshes, rivers and lands. Civilizations also looked upward to the stars and planets, eclipses, meteors and shooting stars for their heavenly indicators. Here on earth the wind direction, cloud formations and thunder and lightning were good guides to what may happen in the future.

Bird omens, in particular, were the subject of very serious study in Greece. Researchers theorize that the reason for this was that in Greek mythology some of their gods and goddesses were believed to have been birds. Birds were particularly sacred and their appearances and movements were of profound significance. The raven, crow, heron, wren, dove, woodpecker and kingfisher were all harbingers of things to come. So, too, were birds of prey - the hawk, eagle and vulture.

Researchers suggest that all cultures believe that some omens may foretell the future, and that it is those omens that become part of an accumulated record, whether oral or written. New events are in turn correlated with past events, and prognostication is born. In time this knowledge becomes accepted as truth, handed down from generation to generation.

TAKE FIVE

In the Atlantic Canada many people believe doing one of these things will keep away evil spirits.

1. Throw salt over your left shoulder.
2. Cross out a single crow or spit at a single crow.
3. Hang a horseshoe over your door.
4. Never put shoes on a table.
5. Put salt at your front door.

TAKE 5 MORE

6. Never bury a woman in black.
7. always make the sign of the cross on a freshly baked loaf of bread.
8. Never sweep dirt out the front door.
9. Never cut your finger or toenails on Sunday.
10. Avoid doing laundry on Sunday.

OUR DAILY BREAD

A crumb of knowledge can go a long way to protecting your family and securing your home.

• When you move into a new house, bring a loaf of bread with you for good luck.

• Never cut a new loaf of bread on both ends. It's bad luck.

Did you know...

that if you think someone may be a witch, lay a broom handle across your threshold. They will not cross but if they do, they will not be able to practice witchcraft?

- To place the sign of the cross upon a freshly-baked loaf of bread is said to bring good luck to the household and will keep evil spirits at bay.

- If you burn a slice of toast, you will hear from a member of your family you have not seen for a while.

- A loaf of bread should never be turned upside down once it's cut or it will bring bad luck.

- To cut bread in an uneven manner is a sign that you have been telling lies.

- When a fisherman is lost overboard, it is customary to place a lit candle on a slice of bread and set it adrift. This, it is said, will comfort the lost crewman.

THE DEVIL MADE ME DO IT

What you can do to keep the devil at bay.

- Don't drink water and look into a mirror at midnight, or you will see the devil.

- Some people fasten horseshoes over their doors for good luck. To keep the devil from entering your house, hang the horseshoe upside down.

Did you know...

that if you paint your door blue, the devil will not enter?

Peter Kelly

Mayor Peter Kelly began his career in public service in 1985 when he was elected Councillor for the Town of Bedford. In 1991 he was elected mayor of Bedford, then in 1995 as Councillor for District 21 - Bedford in the newly amalgamated Halifax Regional Municipality (HRM). He was elected Mayor of HRM in 2000, re-elected in 2004 and again 2008.

I am astounded at how superstitious we all are. Here are a few I have heard over the years:

- Come aboard a ship with your right foot first for good luck. You're also less prone to injury.

- Never kill a gull or a seabird because it's bad luck and means a bad catch.

- Never launch a boat on a Friday for the same reason

- When dolphins swim alongside a ship, it means a safe journey.

- When leaving port never look back.

- Never wipe your hands on the same towel or you'll end up in a fight.

- If you play cards on Sunday you play with the devil.

- You should always leave a house by the same door you came in.

- Of course, everyone knows to throw salt over their shoulder to ward off bad luck. It stems from the time Judas spilled the salt at the Last Supper, branding him as the betrayer of Jesus.

- It is said that if you cut your finger or toe nails on Sunday, the Devil will follow you around for an entire week.

- Putting salt on the doorstep of a new house will keep the devil from entering.

- You can chase away the devil if you throw salt in a fire.

- Avoid meeting a cat at midnight. You just may meet the devil.

- If you place a mirror at your front door, the devil will see his reflection and will not enter. This was also said to work on witches.

THE WITCHING HOUR

Be leery of those who come to call.

- It is said that witches hate brass, so to prevent a witch from making your cow's milk dry-up, hang a brass bell around the animal's neck.

- If you think a witch is visiting your house, stick a woman's hair pin in the corner of your door casings. If you do not have a hair pin, a fork will work the same magic.

- Placing needles around the house is also a good way to fend off witches.

- To protect yourself from witches you should always wear blue because witches do not like blue.

Rodney MacDonald

Rodney MacDonald, a young Cape Breton professional fiddle player and Phys. Ed. Teacher, was selected by his party to replace retiring premier John Hamm as leader of the Nova Scotia Progressive Conservative Party in 2006, making him the youngest premier in Nova Scotia history. Rodney MacDonald also served as Nova Scotia Tourism Minister from 1999 to 2006. He represented the riding of Inverness but following the Conservative defeat in the June 2009 provincial election, MacDonald resigned his seat and is now in private life.

While I am not a superstitious person, I am always interested to hear the many and varied superstitions that have been shared within communities or within professions. The fishery, of course, has many. I was amazed to learn that having someone on board with mittens that were not white could send a captain back to shore to begin a voyage again. The journey would only resume after the colored mittens were disposed of. That said, the spring that I worked on a lobster boat, I always wore white gloves.

The superstition of rocking an empty chair in the house could also be a harbinger of death or perhaps a visit by a ghost. Of course, by breaking a mirror you are supposed to have seven years bad luck. Again, the bad luck might come more immediately in the form of injury from the broken glass itself.

There was also the thought that if you cross over a body of water, the devil cannot cross after you. This has been used in association with stories where a horse pulling a wagon is spooked and races forward but settles after crossing a bridge, because presumably the devil was left behind on the other side of the bridge.

I love these stories and whether you believe or don't believe in these superstitions, the history of their origin fascinates everybody.

- Placing mercury in the barn will protect the animals from the powers of a witch.

- Burning horse or dog hair is said to be a good way to repel witches.

- If you place a mirror at your front door, a witch will see her reflection and will not enter. This was also said to work on the Devil.

- Hang a reflective bulb in your window and if the witch see her reflection causing her to flee. This is called a witch's ball.

- Dog's are extremely sensitive to witches and if they bark uncontrollably at someone, she just might be a witch.

- It was once thought that people with freckles, red hair or odd colored eyes were witches.

A LITTLE ADDED PROTECTION

Discourage witches from sitting a spell.

- Sprinkle salt around your garden, a witch will not enter.

- Plant rosemary by your doorstep to keep the witches from entering your home.

- Bring clover into your house to protect yourself from witches.

- The sound of a bell ringing will drive away a witch. This is also true of evil spirits.

- Bury a knife under your doorstep, a witch will not cross your threshold because she does not like cold steel.

- Or you could lay a pair of scissors at the threshold of a door with the points facing outward.

- Hanging crosses or animal horns in the trees around your property will keep the witches at bay.

- It is said that witches hate brass so to prevent a witch from making your cow's milk dry, up, hang a brass bell around the animal's neck.

Notes

Notes

Notes

Notes